D1577755

DANCE OF
DESIRE

89-GO11

DANCE OF DESIRE

Tragic passion behind New Orleans' festive mask

Janet G. Go

Also by the author:

"Where America's Day Begins, Confessions of a Jungle Journalist," 1998, The National Writers Press, Aurora, Colorado. ISBN: 1-88100-100-7, LOCN: 98-66731.

"Micronesia Visitor Guide," 1969, Hawaii Business Publishing Corporation, Honolulu, Hawaii.

ACKNOWLEDGMENTS

M Y deep gratitude goes to editor *extraordinaire* Jane Albritton for her professional editing and personal encouragement.

Thanks also to my New Orleans friends, Dolores and Mary, who watched this tragedy evolve. We will always remember Remy, fondly, with love.

Ye who believe in affection that hopes, and endures, and is patient, Ye who believe in the beauty and strength of woman's devotion, List to the mournful tradition still sung by the pines of the forest; List to a Tale of Love in Acadie, home of the happy.

From Henry Wadsworth Longfellow's "Evangeline."

PROLOGUE

During my years as a journalist and travel writer, I've climbed Haleakala at sunrise, admired the majesty of Notre Dame Cathedral in the fog, skied across frozen lakes in Norway, bicycled in a May Day race in Rome, and been stranded at midnight atop Victoria Peak after the last funicular had descended into dazzling Hong Kong.

New Orleans is the only city I've seen that exceeds my preconception of it. My early impressions were gleaned, I'll admit, from newspaper accounts of Mardi Gras parades and Tennessee Williams' plays, "A Streetcar Named Desire" and "Cat on a Hot Tin Roof." New Orleans is full of mystery, of sound and fury, sensual cuisine, intoxicating beverages, fiery music and dance, hurricanes, floods, and Blanche Du Bois.

Beyond the French quarter, another side of New Orleans spreads up and down the Mississippi River and the freeways where real people go about their workaday lives in ordinary neighborhoods.

This story is true, but some scenes have been fictionalized for dramatic purposes. The crime was nourished by New Orleans. If the characters were exported to another city in another state, the story might not have happened, at least not in the same way.

Quite a few people had a part in this story, but they will never tell it.

This story is Vince's really. He should be the one to tell it, but he won't.

It's also Angela's story, but she won't tell it.

And it's Remy's story, too. Of course it is, but she *can't* tell it.

At first I wasn't sure I should tell this story, but I can't *not* tell it.

CHAPTER ONE

"What *is* a shellfish boil?" I asked.

"It's a Cajun tradition, a picnic," Remy Rawley snickered. "People stuff themselves on creatures of the sea, and spicy sauce drips down their elbows."

"Whew. Sounds messy."

"Oooh, but it's fun," said Ellen O'Reilly.

On that sultry Friday morning in late September, the Mississippi River steamed like a kettle of boiling water. The muggy air was thick with a malodorous melange of brine, sewage, and petroleum that painted the water a shade of *café au lait*.

Remy, Ellen, and I, Grace Hill, were crossing the Mississippi River on a Navy motorlaunch. We were heading for the annual shellfish boil hosted by the Navy Facility for its employees and families. The Facility's headquarters sat on the bank of the Mississippi in New Orleans. The civilian personnel and logistics offices and the supply depot were located in Algiers, across the river from headquarters and directly opposite the French Quarter.

We three women were among headquarters' employees, spouses, and children who were riding across the muddy river to the picnic. The boat's engine throbbed as the young WAVE skipper expertly maneuvered the small boat up and over wakes, created by a passing oil tanker registered in Nigeria, a cargo ship flying a Panama flag, and the *Natchez* paddlewheeler.

Remy leaned on the railing of the boat and brushed back a lock of her copper-colored hair. She removed her Dior sunglasses, revealing green, amber-flecked eyes. She wiped her forehead and cheeks with a Kleenex and put her glasses back on the bridge of her perspiring nose.

"I'm sweating like a stevedore," I said as I stood beside Remy at the rail. I wiped my forehead. "New Orleans sure is hot and humid. It's like being smothered beneath a damp blanket in Guam. I'll bet the temperature is at least ninety-five degrees and the humidity is the same."

New Orleans' climate is warm and as soft as a baby. Things grow quickly here. Men move slowly in the languid tranquility of this city. The tempo is always summertime, a slow-motion leisurely waltz.

This was the last Friday of my first month in New Orleans. I was still intrigued by the city- and riverscape. I glanced to the right, where the narrow Mississippi curves in a crescent around New Orleans, a jewel set five feet below the river's high levees. New Orleans is a scimitar-shaped city fitted into the curve of the great river. Moss hangs from trees like beards, and alligators float in the tea-colored water of bayous. The nearby Gulf of Mexico is a cornucopia overflowing with shrimp so large a man can hold only two in his cupped palm, oysters as large as cakes and sweet as honey, and fish of every kind.

Downriver, the banks are dotted with warehouses and concrete piers. The city's location has made it the greatest port in the South and one of the busiest ports in the United States. Here, international ships load products from the heartland of America to carry to world ports. The city's population has a special tang, rising as it did around deep water and docks and ships from far away.

As the shuttle boat tied up at the Algiers dock, the spicy aroma of shellfish floating in the air teased our noses and palates. We walked from the pier a short distance over a sandy path, leading through a field of thick grass, to the Navy's recreation area.

On the way, several Navy pilots raced ahead of us. One flyboy winked as he passed us. "Hey, Red. How're you doin'?" He ogled Remy.

"A-okay." Remy smiled at him. "He's one of the admiral's aides," she whispered to me.

Navy cooks had spent the morning boiling water in ten-gallon kettles atop three gas stoves. When the water was boiling, they added halved corncobs, baby new potatoes, small whole onions, crawfish, crabs, and shrimp. The cooks had spiked the kettles of goodies with Louisiana Crab and Shrimp Boil, a concoction of peppercorns, bay leaves, salt, garlic, vinegar, Cayenne pepper, and lemon juice. One kettle was filled with hot dogs and smoked sausage, especially cooked for the kids.

A dozen tables with wooden benches had been placed under two large pavilions to shelter employees and their families from the hot sun. Each table was set with a pile of bib-sized paper napkins, cocktail sauce, Tabasco sauce, and loaves of French bread.

The pavilions were packed with civilian and Navy bookkeepers, file clerks, secretaries, staff writers, editors, admirals' aides, captains, commanders, master chiefs, and assorted family members. Navy personnel, who had changed out of their starched white uniforms to shorts and T-shirts, were sloshing elbow-deep in the delicacies of the sea.

We three women appropriated places on a long bench at one of the tables. We spread out to save room for Remy's and Ellen's husbands, who were to join us later.

"I'll grab some critters before they get away." Remy uncurled her long bare legs from under the bench and stood up, stretching to a generous five-foot-nine-inches tall.

Remy, secretary to the Facility's rear admiral, had a finely sculpted face, a wide forehead, high cheekbones, and a full mouth. Those who did not know her thought she was of an indeterminable age, over forty, they guessed. Actually, she was 55, as smooth as Cognac.

She wore a loose, light orange shift that came to just above her knees. Its low V-neck hinted at her firm breasts. She wore sandals, revealing her toenails painted to match the three coats of copper polish on her inch-long fingernails, which in turn matched her short, curled-under bob. She would have felt naked without the gold chain round her neck, a gold necklace with a diamond heart dangling in her cleavage, gold and diamond studs in her pierced ears, a diamond-encrusted wedding band, and gold wristlet and anklet.

Remy elbowed through a cluster of men, women, and kids who were scooping up claws, tails, and shells like greedy alligators snapping at nutria in the bayous. Within minutes the tabletop, heaped with a mass of shrimp, crawfish, and veggies, was bare.

Returning, Remy plopped the overflowing paper plate onto the table and sat down.

I helped myself to shrimps, an ear of corn, an onion, and a potato. When Ellen placed a crawfish on my plate, I asked, "Isn't this lobster? How do I eat it?"

"We call them crawfish," said Ellen. "Do as the Cajuns do. Squeeze the tail and suck the head. Like this." Ellen squeezed the tail of the red crustacean, peeled off its hard shell, twisted out the juicy meat, and took a bite. She didn't suck the head.

I followed her example. "Mmmm...delicious." I dipped a piece of crawfish into a fiery mixture of cocktail sauce and Tabasco.

Ellen O'Reilly, a five-foot-three-inch natural blonde, was as pretty as an Irish porcelain doll. She had pale skin, dark blue eyes, and delicate cheek bones. Her extremely fair skin revealed the faint bluish patterns of veins. Her pleasant face was wrinkle-free, smooth as a baby's belly, and she didn't need much makeup. Though her hair was showing a few grey streaks, she didn't look her 64 years. She was a descendant of the lace-curtained Irish, two-toilet Irish, not the shanty Irish. She was the kind of woman a man would take home to mother. She always dressed modestly in outfits similar to the pale green, light-weight pants suit she wore to the picnic.

Ellen was secretary to the Navy captain in charge of plans and operations. As she had worked at the Facility for almost forty years, she had become the organization's unofficial historian. She was curious, or nosy some fellow workers would say, and she kept abreast of all the office gossip.

"How long did it take you to organize this shellfish boil?" I asked Ellen, who put her heart and soul into her role as social hostess for the Facility when she organized official luncheons and parties.

"Not long. I had plenty of help from the cooks at the Facility. I just had to distribute invitations to the staff and employees and their families. Everyone looks forward to this annual event."

"Come 'n get it," one cook yelled as he dumped another ten-gallon kettleful of food on the picnic table. The boiling water dribbled between the wooden slats onto the dirt below.

Remy, Ellen, and I dashed to the table. The Facility's rear admiral put his arm around Remy's shoulders and helped her load food onto her plate. I ducked under the arm of a tall Ensign and grabbed a plateful of goodies.

Back at the table, we wasted no time relishing the delicious morsels. Soon our chins, hands, arms, and elbows were dripping with the spicy liquid.

"This is finger-lickin' good," I licked my fingers. "Eating with your fingers is sort of primitive, as sensual as a Roman orgy. This food beats the heck out of the usual Navy chow; you know, beans, hot dogs, cole slaw, and corn bread."

Jacob Owings, the editor of the Facility's monthly newspaper, and my new boss, approached the table. "I couldn't resist sitting with you three beautiful women." He winked and sat down between Remy and me. Jacob was bald, with brown eyes, and the squat build of a wrestler.

Remy laughed and poked Jacob in his side with her elbow. "You've got a line as long as the bridge across the Mississippi."

"Don't you love it?" Jacob grinned.

"Couldn't your wife make it here today?" I asked him.

"No, she had to work this afternoon." The couple lived in Slidell, a small town near the border of Louisiana and Mississippi, close to the O'Reillys' home.

"Well, Grace, what do you think of New Orleans and your first shellfish boil?" Jacob asked.

"I love New Orleans. It's all I expected and more."

"Yeah. New Orleans isn't just a city," Jacob said. "It's a wild gumbo, a melting pot of music, food, and people."

"Very poetic, boss. This shellfish boil reminds me of a Hawaiian luau or a Guamanian fiesta. Just as messy and just as much fun. But I'm melting in this heat! The Jacuzzi in my hotel felt cooler than the outdoor swimming pool."

In mid-afternoon, Dan Rawley and Alex O'Reilly arrived. Although they came in separate cars, they met in the parking lot and walked together to the pavilions.

When Jacob saw the husbands approaching, he stood up and greeted them. After shaking hands with the men, Jacob went to sit at another table. "See you gals Monday."

Dan bent his six-foot frame down to kiss Remy on the cheek. "Hi, honey."

"Hi sweetie." Remy smiled at Dan. "I'd like you to meet Grace Hill. She's working with Jacob."

Dan shook my hand with a firm grip, smiled, and said in a velvet drawl, "Welcome to N'awlins."

Alex plopped down beside Ellen. When she introduced me to him, he grunted and relit the cigar dangling from his florid lips.

"I'm hungry. I'll go get something to eat," said Dan. Remy started to get up. "Let me get it, honey."

"That's okay. I can do it."

Ellen patted Alex on the hand. "I'll fix you a plate, dear." She followed Dan.

"Bring me a beer, Dan," Alex called as Dan went to the food table. Alex spoke with a harsh accent, similar to a Brooklyn or Boston accent.

Dan returned, balancing a plate of food in one hand and two cans of ice-cold beer in the other. He handed Alex a beer and then sat down between Remy and me.

Ellen came back with a plate heaped with food for Alex. He grunted a thanks, took a sip of beer, smoothed one suspender strap, and belched as though he were trying out for Henry the Eighth's stand-in. He was a short, rotund man with quickly vanishing grey hair. A retired oil rig foreman, Alex's face was an Irish roadmap. He was a distant cousin of the Irishman O'Reilly who was governor of New Orleans in the 1800s. Alex's father was a third generation Irishman who had once loaded cotton bales on the wharves in the Irish Channel. The Mississippi River had brought many immigrants to New Orleans, including Alex's ancestors, who arrived from the British Isles in the 18th century.

"Have you seen all the tourist sights in the French Quarter?" Dan asked me.

I put down an ear of corn and wiped my fingers on a paper napkin. "Oh yes, I'm your quintessential first-time visitor. I walked down Pirate's Alley, past the Cabildo, to Jackson Square, which reminded me of Paris. I loved wandering through the French Market on Decatur Street. The variety of fruit and vegetables is so colorful, like a Matisse painting. A few blocks farther, I felt the ghosts of Blanche Du Bois and Stanley Kowalski hovering around me as I gazed at the Streetcar Named Desire. The streetcar looks so lonely and dilapidated parked on the deserted tracks. I could barely make out the faded word 'Desire' on the front windshield."

"Where did you eat?"

"I stopped by the Café du Monde for *café au lait* and beignets. They were delicious, but when I finished eating, my blouse and skirt looked like I had been in a snowstorm of powdered sugar. And I went to the Desire Oyster Bar on Bourbon Street. Since it was August, I hesitated about ordering oysters, but the waiter assured me that the oysters were excellent. I ordered a half dozen. When he brought a metal tray heaped with ice-cold raw oysters I was surprised to count seven. He said that the seventh oyster was a little *lagniappe*."

Dan laughed. "That's a N'awlins' custom—a little something extra."

"That's like a baker's dozen, eh? Anyway, the oysters were delicious."

"This business about eating oysters only in a month with an

'r' in it is an old myth," Dan said. "It stems from the days before refrigeration. The oysters caught in August are, in fact, some of the most flavorful and the saltiest of the year."

Dan turned to Remy. "Vince and Angela Santorini would be right at home with this feast. Too bad they can't get on the base."

Remy explained to me that the Santorinis were long-time friends. "Vince is bartender at Rex Rampart's bar in the Quarter."

"Vince and his wife are Italians, born in New Orleans. He's cute, as cuddly as a teddy bear," Remy winked at Dan.

"More huggable than me, sweetie?"

Remy smiled. "Of course not, dear."

"Does Angela still drink too much?" Ellen asked.

Dan and Remy both nodded.

"I worry about her. It's a good thing she doesn't drive anymore," said Ellen.

"Sometimes I think Vince is too easy on her, not helping her face her drinking problem," Dan said.

"She's a pleasant drunk, though," said Remy. "And can she cook. We have brunch with Vince and Angela every Sunday." She turned to me. "You'll have to join us some time."

"I'd like that. I can't believe everyone is so friendly. I feel right at home." I had moved dozens of times in my 48 years, but nowhere did I feel more at home than in New Orleans.

After lunch, some of the enlisted men and officers played softball, women chatted, and kids kicked a soccer ball around the park, which comprised a softball diamond, volleyball court, and a track oval.

Around three-thirty, the picnic broke up. The cooks and helpers wanted to clean up the mess before they went home at four-fifteen. The Facility's civilian and Navy personnel didn't work much overtime. Duty here was considered duck soup. If you didn't miss too many work days and kept your nose clean, you could be sure of a promotion or at least a plush job until you retired.

I rode home with the Rawleys, since we lived in the same apartment complex in East New Orleans.

In the Facility's parking lot, Remy opened the car door. "Wow!" The heat struck us like an oven, warmed by the summer sun that frequently cracked windshields.

"Give me a few minutes." Dan got into the car, started the engine, and turned on the air-conditioner. Soon, he said, "Now you two ladies can get in."

Dan drove across the river and onto Interstate 10. He turned off the interstate at the Chef Menteur off-ramp and drove to Morrison Road.

When Dan parked at the Kenilworth Apartments, Remy invited me in for a drink. I accepted, eager to compare my one-bedroom unit with their two-bedroom apartment.

Dan ran around to open the car doors and helped us out. Then he walked to the side of the building and picked a few tufts of grass from the lawn.

"What's he doing?"

"Gathering a few blades of grass for Pooh, our Persian cat."

Pooh met us in the foyer of the apartment. A burnt orange carpet led into the livingroom, furnished with an orange sofa, flanked by an entertainment center with TV, stereo, and shelves crammed with records and tapes. Across the room were two overstuffed orange chairs with a lamp table between. In one corner of the livingroom was a white baby grand piano, surrounded by a leather counter and bar stools. Behind was a fully stocked bar.

The apartment walls were almost obscured by paintings, high-lighted by picture lamps. There were oil paintings of a French Quarter patio and garden and a sunset beach scene, plus an assort-ment of cat and clown prints.

"We got this last weekend." Remy pointed to the oil portrait hanging above the sofa. "We had it done for our 20th wedding anniversary by an artist friend who works in Jackson Square."

"It's a good likeness." I gazed at the life-sized portrait of the smiling couple.

Dan went to the bar to mix a pitcher of martinis, and Remy

went into the kitchen. As they passed one another, they patted each other's rear end.

I sat down on the sofa and looked around the room. Every wall, tabletop, and etagere was crammed with clown figurines, music boxes, Mardi Gras masks, tragedy and comedy masks, and Mickey and Minnie Mouse figures. The walls of the foyer and halls leading to the bedrooms held pictures of jazz clarinetist Pete Fountain, when he had a full head of black hair, and Rex Rampart, leader of the Razzy Dazzy Jazzy band.

"Looks like you've been to Disneyland often."

"Yes, Dan and I love Disneyland and Disney World. Every time I visit my daughter in Los Angeles, I take my granddaughters to Disneyland," Remy called from the kitchen.

"You should see the big Mickey Mouse telephone beside our bed. It's two feet tall." Dan handed us the martinis; then he relaxed in his favorite chair.

"You must like clowns a lot," I said, counting at least a dozen clown figurines and paintings.

"Yes. They make me happy."

"You know, the Mardi Gras masks of comedy and tragedy remind me of life, the sad and happy times," I said.

"Well, guess that's true," Dan said.

"You have quite a collection."

Dan laughed. "That's Remy's department. I just pay the bills." He was good-looking, with a thick crop of wavy graying hair. He was a Southern gentleman, intelligent and soft-spoken, a gracious man in the old New Orleans tradition. One who would stop on his way to a fire at his own house to retrieve a lady's dropped handkerchief.

Remy brought in a tray with three plates. One plate was piled high with crackers topped with smoked salmon and olives, and the other dishes were filled with chips and mixed nuts. She placed the tray on the coffee table in front of me and sat down on Dan's lap and pecked his cheek. When Pooh meowed at Dan's feet and rolled her blue eyes at him, Remy got up to get cocktail napkins from the kitchen. Dan's eyes followed her hungrily, as if he couldn't believe that such a paragon was actually his wife.

Pooh jumped onto Dan's lap and purred as her master stroked her silky coat.

"Pooh rules the house." Remy returned to the livingroom and gave us each a napkin. She sat down on the sofa, draping herself as if she were posing for "Playboy."

Strains of the tune "Tangerine" ran through my mind, the song made famous by Jimmy Dorsey about the siren with her eyes of wine and lips as bright as flame and flirty orange fashions. She was known to all the men across the Argentine, as the song goes.

"Were you born in New Orleans?" I asked Dan.

"No, but I spent my teens here. After I retired from the Air Force, Remy and I moved here. I'm working for the city's historic preservation committee. We're renovating the U. S. Mint, turning it into a museum."

"How interesting. You know, you're the happiest married couple I've ever known. You seem to be perfectly in sync. I feel good just being with you love birds."

"We're so lucky," Remy said. "After twenty years of marriage, we're still in love. In fact, it's better than ever." She winked at Dan. "Were you ever married?"

"Yes, unfortunately," I snorted. "Three times. All to losers. One a transvestite and another a liar. My third, last, and longest marriage was to an Oriental. I think he married me to get U.S. citizenship. Guess I'm unlucky in love."

After a few more minutes of pleasant conversation and two martinis, I stood up. "I'd better get home while I could still make it. Thanks for the ride and the drinks."

"You're welcome here anytime," said Remy, walking me to the door.

"See you Monday. Have a nice weekend."

As I walked the short distance to my apartment, I felt like I was floating on cloud nine. I congratulated myself for taking the job and moving to New Orleans. I was smitten with New Orleans.

The queen city is a joyous, diverse blend of music, food, and fun where there is always time for pleasure. Like characters in a book who influence the lives of its readers, the city shapes the lives of its citizens.

The news business had taught me that every living being experiences passion and fear, love and hatred. There is a story, often dark, dangerous, sometimes evil but always compelling, in every human heart and, perhaps, behind the beautiful mask of New Orleans.

CHAPTER TWO

After a chilly autumn, oaks were still green-leafed and trailed with ivy. Winters lasted three weeks at most. That winter, icy winds blew down from Lake Pontchartrain and up from the river. It was the kind of January that no one talks about in New Orleans. Ice appeared on the surfaces of open ditches, while trees, bushes, and tender fronds of banana trees were scarred brown with frost. When the weak sun peeked through the white clouds, it warmed my spirit but not the frosty air that dug into my bones. People with rosy cheeks darted about with their frozen fists in their pockets. I had lived in tropical Pacific islands for twenty years, and winter would take some getting used to.

The Navy Facility held its annual Christmas party and, before I knew it, the New Year had begun. Before the holidays, I was busy hunting for an apartment. Remy suggested I ask whether there was a vacancy at Kenilworth Apartments in East New Orleans where she and Dan lived.

Luckily, there was a one-bedroom apartment available and my household goods arrived from Guam just in time for me to move into the second-floor unit. I had a small balcony that overlooked a man-made lake around which three dozen brick buildings were situated. Wooden fishing piers dotted the shoreline, outlined by a dirt path shaded by palms. Joggers pranced around the path, ducks waddled on shore and begged for bread crumbs, and fish jumped out of the water.

The Kenilworth complex looked like standard government or prison structures minus a barbed-wire fence, about two or three steps above the housing projects in downtown New Orleans and outlying parishes. Shortly before I moved in, the complex had been designated a Housing and Urban Development area. Black families who had been living in substandard housing, or were even homeless, moved in.

The complex was well connected by bus to downtown New Orleans. Occasionally, I rode to work with Betty, an accountant at the Facility who also lived at Kenilworth, or Dan and Remy. However, I usually took the bus because I didn't want to be a burden to my new friends. I had sold my ten-year-old Ford Maverick before I left Guam, and I had to save money to buy another car.

On a Wednesday evening in the second week in January, I invited Dan and Remy to my apartment to celebrate Dan's sixtieth birthday.

"It smells like the Far East in here," said Dan, as he and Remy stepped into my living-dining room. "Something's spicy."

"It's my old standby, chicken curry." I had spent the day cooking the curry, which I served with rice, flat bread, and seven "boys": bowls of mango chutney, peanuts, raisins, coconut, tiny shrimp, chopped green onions, and yogurt raita.

"Would you do the honors, Dan?" I pointed to bottles of vodka and vermouth and a jar of olives on the kitchen counter.

"Sure," he winked. "That's my job."

After we'd settled down in the livingroom, Remy asked, "How do you like your apartment?"

"It's great. I could hardly wait to get out of that Quarter hotel. It was convenient, but it was showing its age."

"What do you mean?"

"The bed was lumpy, the carpeting and drapes were faded, the toilet seat was broken. At night I could hear catcalls from drunken guests on the other side of the thin walls. But I didn't mind. It was only for a week. I was glad when Betty drove me to Kenilworth to look at her apartment. Then I went to the manager's office and asked if there was a vacancy. Lucky for me, this place was empty and I moved in. My household goods arrived from Guam a few days later, so it worked out very well."

We made small talk over two martinis, then we sat down at the table to eat.

"This is delicious," said Remy. "Where did you learn to make curry? In India?"

"No. I've never been there, but I've sailed on P&O ships across the Pacific. Curry is one of their special dishes. Many of the crew and cooks were Indian."

"We've never taken a cruise, but we're thinking of sailing to London next Christmas."

"It's the only way to go," I said. "What ship are you taking?"

"We thought we'd like to take the *Queen Elizabeth 2*."

"That's a great ship. I sailed on the first *Queen Elizabeth* from Cherbourg to New York in 1952. Those were the days of separate classes on ships. The *QE2* is now all one class. You'll have a ball."

For dessert, I served a fruit compote and opened a bottle of champagne.

Remy lifted her champagne flute and it tilted, almost spilling onto the white linen tablecloth. "Oops. My arthritis is acting up again. Anyway, here's to you, sweetheart. May you have another sixty years." She leaned over to kiss Dan on the cheek.

"Where did you two meet?" Grace asked.

"In Budapest," said Dan.

"We fell in love at first sight at the Air Force Officers' Club," said Remy. "We couldn't help ourselves. Dan was divorced, but I was still married. When my husband found out about Dan and me, he gave me an amicable divorce. Dan and I were married immediately. That was twenty years ago." She held Dan's hand in hers. "I married him because he's absolutely devoted to me. He treats me like a queen." She giggled.

Dan reached over to Remy and kissed her cheek. "I love you."

"And if God is willing, I will love you better after death."

"Don't talk like that. I'll be around to take care of you for another twenty years," Dan laughed. "If I'm not here, who'll keep you in line? And buy you diamonds?"

"You'll both be around for a long time, I'm sure. You're young." To change the subject, I asked Dan, "How's the Mint restoration coming along?"

"Fine. Did you know that it was built in 1835 while Andrew Jackson was president? It used to coin both U.S. and Confederate money. When the restoration's finished, the Mint will be part of the Louisiana State Museum, and it will house historic Mardi Gras and New Orleans jazz exhibits."

When they rose to leave, Dan hugged me. "Thanks for a great birthday dinner."

"We'll have many more." As I melted into his bear hug, I felt as safe as a ship in a snug harbor.

"Thanks, Grace. We had a lovely time." Remy hugged me. "I almost forgot to ask you. Would you like to join us to watch the Mardi Gras parade? We're going to a restaurant on St. Charles Avenue, right on the parade route. The O'Reillys and Santorinis will be there too."

"I'd love to. I've wanted to go to Mardi Gras since I was in college. This will be the first time I've ever seen a Mardi Gras parade."

"Good. I'll let you know the details later."

After Remy and Dan left, I cleared the table and thought about them. They had love, security, and the good life. When they were together, a radiant nimbus hovered around them. Remy seemed to be one of those people who attract love and sex easily, like a strong wind to which she had only to turn her face.

During February, Mardi Gras fever rears its hedonic head. New Orleans puts on her best face during the garish splendor of Mardi Gras, French for Fat Tuesday, probably the world's largest annual celebration. Mardi Gras is the spirit and soul of the city.

On a cool, drizzly Saturday afternoon in East New Orleans, I put on a sweater, a Mardi Gras woolen cap I bought in the French

Quarter, and my old ski gloves and jacket. As I walked the five blocks
to Haynes Boulevard on the lakefront, I shivered in the cold, humid
air. The boulevard was lined on both sides with people braving the
unusually cold weather to watch the neighborhood parade.

For me, the star of the parade was the Anheuser-Busch team of
eight shaggy-hoofed Clydesdale horses trotting down the boulevard. After the parade ended, I quickly walked home to make a hot
toddy to warm my toes.

The next morning I read in the *Times Picayune* that the Cly-
desdales had caught pneumonia while marching along the
lakefront in the wintry weather. Unfortunately, they were too
sick to stay for the Fat Tuesday parade, and they were sent back to
their home stables.

Remy and Dan had invited me to watch Mardi Gras in style.
Accustomed to the comforts of life, the Rawleys couldn't refuse an
offer from Ye Olde Spaghetti Factory on St. Charles Avenue, located a block uptown from Canal Street.

For $17.95 a person, patrons could park in the restaurant's back
lot and have a reserved table inside in one of the dozen quaint trolley
cars, where they would be served a complete breakfast and substantial
lunch. Drinks and snacks were extra, but the convenience of having
warm rest rooms and a cozy bar was worth the price of admission.

Around 7:30 a.m. on Fat Tuesday, the Rawleys picked me up
and we drove to get Vince and Angela Santorini, who lived in a
double shotgun house three miles from Kenilworth.

Shortly after we arrived at the restaurant, Ellen and Alex
O'Reilly joined us. A waiter showed us to a table in our private
car. Angela, Vince, Remy, and Dan sat on one side of the table,
with Vince and Remy in the center, and Alex, Ellen, and I sat
opposite them.

While we were devouring delicious Eggs Benedict and eye-
opening Bloody Marys, I glanced across the table at the Santorinis.

Vince was a short, Italian man with dark good looks. He spoke
with a heavy New Orleans blue-collar accent, which is closer to
the speech of Brooklyn than to the deep south. He had black wavy

hair, big brown eyes with long black lashes, thin shoulders, and a lean body. He wore the pleasant expression of an Italian singer about to open a show for a comedian.

Angela Santorini had the purpuric complexion of a spirits-lover. Also Italian, she had a round face and an angelic smile; she appeared to be the epitome of her name. She wore her thick hennaed black hair in a bouffant style.

Ellen said she and Alex had watched the parades of the Krewe of Troy and Krewe of Slidellians near their home in Slidell. I told them about the Clydesdale horses getting sick in the lakefront parade.

"Where did the word krewe come from?" I asked.

Ellen put her fork down and explained, "It was coined by the Mistick Krewe of Comus in 1857 to give the club's name an Old English flavor."

"Those posters are beautiful." I pointed to dozens of framed documents that decorated one wall of the restaurant.

"Those are Mardi Gras proclamations," said Ellen. "They began as newspaper advertisements proclaiming that peace and prosperity of the city would be assured by organizing the wandering maskers on Mardi Gras into a procession on Canal Street. Incidentally, masking is allowed by law only one day each year, on Mardi Gras. Some sixty parades are held before Mardi Gras, and Bacchus, Endymion...."

"Stifle it." Alex glared at his wife.

Ellen looked down at her plate.

I snickered to myself, but felt sorry for Ellen. I hadn't heard that put-down since Archie Bunker went off the air.

We heard police sirens screaming outside.

"The parade's comin'. I'll go see how close they are." Dan went out to the street.

Soon the boom-boom-boom of bass drums filtered into the crowded restaurant.

"That's the march call for every redblooded New Orleanian," said Remy, as she leaned against Vince's shoulder and winked at him. Remy and Vince were very cozy, I thought, but no one payed any attention to their behavior.

"They'll be rollin' soon," Dan said as he returned to finish his breakfast.

The restaurant's gallery could be reached through French doors from the bar on the second floor. Here, patrons had bird's-eye views of the parade without rubbing elbows with the street crowds. Remy, Dan, Vince, Ellen, and Alex went to watch from the gallery.

Angela signaled the waiter to bring her another Bloody Mary, then stood up. "Come outside with me, Grace. You've got to see Mardi Gras the right way."

Drink in hand, Angela led me to the sidewalk, where people were huddled a dozen deep from curb to wall on the banquette on both sides of St. Charles Avenue. They pushed and jostled for the best positions along the curb, and some in front sat on folding chairs. Fathers held ladders for their kids to climb on, to see over the crowd, while others held toddlers on their shoulders. Even before the parade began, excited children were squealing with delight, and adults were chattering about last year's parade, wondering if this year's parade could top that.

The people on the sidewalks and balconies cheered at the sight of the policemen on horseback and motorcycles, ten abreast, who cleared a path for the marchers. Behind the police vanguard were Veterans of Foreign Wars on horseback and in open carriages.

The carnival captain appeared on a special float at the head of the procession. Next came the officers, the king, maids, and dukes on floats carrying riding members.

The title float, pulled by a pair of brawny mules, was an enormous papier mache version of the Boeuf Gras, French for fatted bull or ox, the ancient symbol of the last meal eaten before the Lenten season of fasting began.

With the flourish of trumpets and crash of cymbals came the Zulu float. Angela explained that the Zulu krewe was founded in 1909 by blue-collar iconoclasts who paraded in the back streets in

African garb and minstrel-show blackface to thumb their noses at Mardi Gras traditions. Zulu adopted its own mythical society in which members elected a mayor, city official, or other "big shot" as their king. Louis Armstrong reigned as Zulu king in 1949. This was the first year that Zulu was allowed to participate in the main parade on Fat Tuesday.

Next came Rex, the King's float that rose to the height of the galleries along the street. His Royal Majesty, Rex, the King of Misrule, was seated high above the crowds, his ermine train cascading down the back of the float. He gracefully swept his scepter over the heads of his loyal subjects.

Rex began as a secretive, high-society organization in 1782. Celebrities were usually invited to ride on Rex floats. They included Bob Hope, Dolly Parton, Wayne Newton, Jackie Gleason, Kirk Douglas, Harry Connick, Jr., and the Beach Boys.

It was proper etiquette for the hoi polloi to holler and beg, as the "aristocrats" on the floats showed their largess by casting trinkets into the crowd.

Angela raised her hands and called, "Throw me something, mister." The maskers tossed beads and doubloons her way. She gave me a few. "Try to catch some. But don't stoop to pick up beads from the sidewalk or street or you'll be trampled to death."

Next came a high school marching band. They played the carnival theme song, "If I Ever Cease to Love," followed by a jazzy rendition of "While We Danced at the Mardi Gras."

Maskers were skilled at sailing strings of glass and plastic beads through the air to people standing on the galleries, and Remy and Ellen caught handfuls of beads and doubloons as they leaned over the restaurant's gallery railing.

Soon I was yelling like a native, "Throw me something, mister." I quickly filled up the cloth bag, with Delta Queen steamboat imprinted on it, that Remy had given me to collect trinkets.

Between floats, private costumed groups danced down the street. I thought the participants, whether on floats or in the audience, looked like they had been up all night imbibing, as is New

Orleans' wont. Couples, loosened by drink, danced in the street to tinpanny syncopation between floats.

"Here comes Pete Fountain," Angela shouted as Pete's Half-Fast Walking Club made a pit stop at the restaurant.

Organized in 1961, Pete's group was one of the most popular of the marching bands. Each year, he and his musicians walked about nine miles, while sipping wine from goatskins. Short, chubby, baldheaded Pete and his entourage wore gaudy beaded costumes and high plumed helmets.

They all went inside the Spaghetti Factory, where they joined the Rawleys and Vince Santorini, who bought them drinks at the bar. Angela and I followed. Angela ordered another Bloody Mary. Vince and Angela first met Pete twenty years earlier, when they owned Evangeline's Desire Bar in the Quarter. Remy and Dan were fans of Pete and owned all of his records and cassettes. Soon, Pete's group moved on down St. Charles Avenue.

A few minutes later, Rex Rampart's Razzy Dazzy Jazzy Marching Band stopped prancing and went into the restaurant. Angela and I followed the band inside. Rex was six-feet one-inch tall, an unusual height among shorter jazz greats like Pete Fountain and Louis Armstrong. Vince worked at Rex's bar, so he knew Rex and his band members intimately. We all toasted a drink before the band moved on. Remy and Dan were great fans of Rex too.

Around 1 p.m., there was a lull in the parade, and we gathered at the table in our private rail car for lunch. Bowls of spicy, steaming Seafood Gumbo and more Bloody Marys fortified us for the afternoon ahead.

"This is so rich. What's in it?" I asked as I spooned up some gumbo.

"Ask Angela. She's the gourmet cook in the group," said Remy.

"You start with a roux, then add onions, garlic, bell pepper, oysters, shrimp, crab, okra, wine, Tabasco sauce, and filé. Come over to the house some time and I'll show you how to make it."

"I'd like that," I nodded. "They sure do let the good times roll here."

"We know how to celebrate," said Vince, downing the remainder of his Bloody Mary. "We can't listen to the music without dancing, and to most of us, liquor means fun." Vince had a smile that could melt the powdered sugar off a beignet.

"Show me a Louisianan and I'll show you someone who can drink even an Irishman under the table," Dan winked at Alex. "People grow up drinking. Saloons are everywhere. A drunk is never arrested unless he's harming other people."

"A drink is a Cajun handshake." Vince pressed his shoulder against Remy. "Isn't that right?"

Remy smiled and nodded.

"I don't trust a man, or a woman, who doesn't drink." Dan finished his Bloody Mary too.

"Oooh." Ellen smiled and patted her husband's hand. "Oooh" was the only four-letter word in Ellen's vocabulary.

Alex guffawed, then relit his fat cigar. I drew back as the smoke drifted my way.

"Happy hours seem to be daily rituals here," I commented.

"What did you expect in a city where Bacchus reigns?" Vince said.

After lunch, I stood up. "I'd like to walk to the French Quarter to see what's happening there. Anyone want to join me?"

They all shook their heads. "No way. Be careful. If you're not back within an hour, we'll send a St. Bernard," Remy joked.

I strolled the couple of blocks to the Quarter, which was off-limits to vehicular traffic during the last few days of the carnival season. The Fire Department had recently banned parading through the French Quarter, though it had been a tradition for 117 years.

The Quarter, or Vieux Carre, the city's heart that never stops beating, is a six- by twelve-block rectangle bordered by the Mississippi River and three 280-year-old streets with flagstoned alleyways and high-walled courtyards.

Narrow Bourbon Street overflowed with a thousand costumed, emblazoned, bespangled people, and plumed and beribboned horses. Everyone was jiggling to the beat of music blaring from bars and balconies. Revelers played trumpets, trombones, flutes, and drums. Partygoers and musicians greeted and hugged each other, strangers or not.

At St. Ann and Bourbon Streets, a crowd had gathered on the corner. "What's going on?" I asked a woman so tall she could see over the spectators.

"It's the annual transvestite beauty contest, honey." She, or he, grinned and winked at me.

Mardi Gras activities are unfettered pagan fun and frivolity before Lent, which had its roots in spring fertility rites and had retained an air of sexuality down through the centuries. The city's municipal code prohibits nudity, but on Mardi Gras, no one cares. I wandered among rowdies, prostitutes, and pickpockets strolling under the crowded balconies. Bare-breasted young women hung over balconies, and on others, fully nude males and females mooned the adoring crowds below.

Another municipal code prohibits an entertainer from wearing the clothing of the opposite sex mingling with the public at a place of entertainment, but transvestites are *de rigueur* in the Vieux Carre on Fat Tuesday. This is a day-long extravaganza of transvestism, female impersonation, and sexual confusion of the first water. Transvestites parade in bright costumes, masks, and hats with bright feathers and carry colorful paper parasols.

I skirted a crowd encircling five small Black boys who were dancing a slap-foot, spasm dance, hoping for a shower of pennies. Turning away, I was stopped by a black-costumed man with a theatrical white mask of comedy. He held out a rose to me and bowed. I accepted, "Thank you."

As I walked back to St. Charles, I passed uniformed policemen who were enjoying the party too. They were there to break up fistfights and to arrest drunks who swung at the cops, brandished a weapon, or tried to break into shop windows.

I joined Angela in front of the restaurant. "D'ya want a drink?" She held up her glass.

"No, thanks."

The Krewe of Argus, a truck parade, inched by. The Elks Orleanians, founded in 1935, was the oldest and largest of the truck krewes, with 92 trucks and 3,000 riders. Following them was the Crescent City truck parade, founded in 1947. Riders tossed purple, green, and gold anodized Crescent City doubloons, as well as printed cups to the crowd.

"Are they real Indians?" I pointed to groups dressed to resemble American Indians in costumes of beads and feathers.

"No. They're Black men. The custom began a century ago. Two famous tribes are the Jefferson Indians and the Wild Tchoupitoulas."

Then the krewes of Jefferson, Elks Gretna, and Elks Jefferson paraded until 5 p.m. At dusk, the streets were lit by flambeaux, naphtha-fueled torches, carried by white-robed Black men.

After the bacchanal, the crowd dispersed quickly, and crews began cleaning the debris.

In the car on the way home, Vince told me, "A successful Mardi Gras is measured by the amount of trash collected by sanitation crews. The total for a 12-day parade season can top 2,000 tons."

"It's not over yet," said Dan. "For some people, the festivities continue at the Municipal Auditorium."

"It used to be held at the French Opera House," Angela interjected.

"What happens there?" I asked.

"The meeting of the courts, where Rex and Comus and their entourages make champagne toasts to signal the end of Carnival."

"The city will be scrubbed, bright-eyed, and bushy-tailed before morning, when families attend Ash Wednesday Mass," said Angela. "At midnight, the season of Lent officially begins."

The spirit of New Orleans is one of pleasure, which is reflected in its motto, "*Laissez les bon temps rouler*," let the good times roll. The people of this city believe devoutly in their right to drink, dance, gamble, make love, and worship God. Most of my new friends were older than I, but they didn't seem to be aging. Did the joy of living keep them young? Had they found the key to the fountain of youth?

CHAPTER THREE

The weeks of Lent brought more frigid winds and gray days. One day it was cold and damp, and the next day the sun rose hot in the clear blue sky. Everyone knew that spring had arrived.

That Friday morning in April was evil with rain and darkness. I was awakened by the loud clapping of thunder, lightning striking overhead, and rain rattling the bedroom window. I squinted at the glow-in-the-dark dial of my bedside clock: 2:25 a.m. There was nothing I could do about the weather, so I rolled over and slept three more hours.

When I got out of bed, washed my face, and dressed for work, I had no sense of impending drama, no inkling of things to come that day.

As I applied my makeup, I examined my reflection in the bathroom mirror. Silver strands were creeping into my brown, mousey-colored hair. My square face reflected my mother's German ancestors, and my light blue eyes had seen much and remembered much in my 48 years, half of which had been spent in newspapering.

After a cup of instant coffee, I locked my apartment door and left the building. Wearing a light raincoat over my blouse and slacks, I opened my umbrella and crossed Morrison road to wait for the bus.

The rain had continued all night long. Its damp scent was piercing and sweet, like an embrace. The skies opened up as though the bottom had ripped out of a paper bag full of water. Usually, rains occur almost every afternoon this time of year. It comes down hard, drenches you, then stops before you know it. Not this storm.

A low-pressure system had moved in from the Gulf of Mexico and dumped heavy rains on New Orleans. This was April, way ahead of the usual rainy season. The rain began suddenly, as it will in southern Louisiana, sweeping up from Algiers and across the low-lying neighborhoods of the city, bringing the damp smell of the river and muddy bayous of the delta.

As I stood almost ankle deep in water waiting for my 6:25 a.m. bus, the low, black-green clouds and dancing veins of lightning rolling north to Lake Ponchartrain made me uneasy. Torrents of rain blew through the streets, thrashed the palm trees, overran the gutters, and filled the tunnel of oak trees on the neutral grounds with gray mist.

The bus arrived right on time and I hopped aboard. I smiled at the driver and greeted the regular riders. Half an hour later on Canal Street in New Orleans, I got off the bus and ducked under the canopy of the Maison Blanche department store to wait for my connecting bus. The rain was coming down heavier. Water was flooding from the street, over the curb, and onto the sidewalks.

I didn't have long to wait before my next bus arrived. Twenty minutes later, I got off the bus at Poland Street and waded through puddles on the sidewalks for four blocks to the Navy Facility, rising high on the banks of the Mississippi River.

As I did every morning, I went to the basement cafeteria, where I usually met Remy and Ellen, and sometimes Dan and Alex, for coffee and biscuits before going to our offices. Dan frequently stopped for breakfast before going to his job. Alex O'Reilly drove Ellen to work, grabbed a cup of coffee, and returned home to Slidell.

That morning, none of the four was in the cafeteria. I was puzzled. Where were they? Were they held up in traffic? When it rained heavily, New Orleans' streets flooded and cars sometimes stalled in the deep potholes.

In the sixth-floor Public Affairs Office, the Navy chiefs and Jacob, my boss, were already at their desks.

I hung my raincoat on the clothes rack, shook my sopping umbrella, folded it, and stowed it in the typewriter well of my battleship-gray metal desk.

"What a miserable morning." I smiled at Jacob.

"Morning."

I was surprised by Jacob's sullen greeting and his ashen face and eyes, usually full of mischief.

I glanced into the next room. Two Navy journalists, the civilian speech writer, and secretary were huddled together around a desk. Their faces pale. This was unusual. On most mornings they discussed, over coffee, what they had done the evening before, told a few off-color jokes, then planned the day's schedule, which might include covering breaking news or a staff meeting with the Public Affairs Officer, our boss.

"They look like they're attending a wake. Who died?"

"Dan Rawley. Early this morning," Jacob answered.

"You've got to be kidding." I didn't believe him. I usually took everything Jacob said with a pinch of salt, sometimes with a whole shaker.

Jacob shook his head. "The admiral's aide told us. Dan had a stroke during the night. He died on the way to the hospital."

"God, I can't believe it." I shook my head. "He and Remy were at my house for dinner three nights ago to celebrate Dan's sixtieth birthday. Remy must be devastated. Dan was her whole life. Is anyone with her now?"

"Angela Santorini called the admiral. So I guess she's with Remy. Ellen O'Reilly found out when she got here half an hour ago. Alex hadn't left yet, so she took annual leave and they drove to Remy's."

Tears clouded my eyes. None of us is prepared for the loss of a loved one, and when the loss comes without warning, the devastation is complete.

"Remy's going to need all her friends to get over Dan's death."

I couldn't concentrate on getting the monthly Navy newspaper to press.

Jacob ran his hand over his bald head. "You and I, and everyone else, will be there for her, Grace."

Around noon, Jacob said, "Why don't you take the afternoon off? I'll go to the print shop. You go see Remy. Give her my sympathy."

"Thanks, boss." When he left to take the camera-ready layout sheets to the printer on Tchoupitoulas Street, I took four hours' annual leave and headed home.

I caught the St. Claude bus, which ran through the French Quarter. Riding the Quarter bus was like visiting a human zoo. There were poor people, lonely people clutching plastic Safeway bags. An old man across the aisle from me wore a stocking cap pulled tight and low over his forehead. He whispered to himself and nodded his head. The woman in front of me reeked of stale beer and tobacco. On a front seat that faced the driver, a street preacher was shouting that everyone of us was going to burn in hell. Sometimes truculent drunks, drug dealers, thugs, whores rode this route. I grew accustomed to the occasional leers from the perverts, and I had perfected the art of no eye contact with these people.

I got off the bus and sloshed up Canal Street to wait for the East New Orleans bus on Rampart Street. I ducked under the porch of one of the brick, three-story buildings of a housing project. I always waited there, despite my fellow workers' warnings not to be alone near these hot-beds of crime. The residents never bothered me.

When the East New Orleans bus arrived, I dashed from the porch and climbed aboard. Through the fogged-up bus window, I saw the gray gloom that had lowered over the city, which appeared to be sinking from the weight of the rain. As we crossed the drawbridge at the Industrial Canal, I noticed that the water almost overflowed its banks. In the darkening afternoon, roaring winds slamdanced trees, causing them to bend, wiggle and touch the ground in weird hulas.

By the time I reached Kenilworth Apartments, the streets looked like a mini-Lake Pontchartrain. Roof gutters overflowed and sheets of rain pummeled to the ground. Black branches of oaks roared loudly as they swayed in the wind and lashed against roofs. The flooding all over New Orleans was almost biblical.

Remy's apartment door was open. Inside, I saw that Vince and Angela, Ellen and Alex were already ensconced with attitude-adjustment drinks. Remy's smooth face was swollen from crying. She wore no makeup.

"I can't believe it. What a shock. I'm so sorry." I hugged Remy. "Jacob sends his condolences."

Soon the admiral's aide and his wife arrived and hugged Remy. The aide carried a large paper bag, which was so wet it was almost falling apart, but it still yielded a tantalizing aroma of po'boys.

"Can I get you a drink? Coffee, tea, or a sandwich?" Remy asked the couple.

"Coffee would be fine," said the aide's wife.

"Regular or N'awlins?"

"For God's sake, Remy, can't you ever stop with the southern hospitality? We can help ourselves." The aide raked his fingers through his thinning hair.

I had forgotten to eat lunch, so I picked up a slice of po'boy from the dining table. Idly, I thought that if I had to choose my "last" meal on earth, I'd opt for an oyster po'boy.

I went into the kitchen to see Angela making a fresh pot of coffee. "Tell me what happened."

"Our phone rang this morning about 2:15. Vince answered it. It was Remy. She said that thunder woke her up and she felt cold because the blanket was off her. When she reached the blanket, she noticed Dan wasn't in bed. She rolled across the bed and saw him lying on the floor, curled up on his right side like a baby. He must have fallen off the bed during the night. The blanket was wrapped around his left arm.

"Remy touched his neck, shoulder, and arm. They were stone cold. His tongue was sticking out and she couldn't feel a pulse on his left wrist. She called 911. When paramedics came, they rushed

Dan to Humana Hospital. Then Remy called us. Of course, we rushed over and drove Remy to the hospital." Angela wiped tears from her eyes.

"What happened next?"

"The doctor told us that Dan had had a stroke. He didn't make it to the hospital. He said he died fast, painlessly. After a while, we took Remy home. I stayed with her all night and called the admiral this morning."

"Who's been taking care of everything?"

"Vince called Remy's daughter, Jacquie Sanchez, and Dan's brothers. The admiral's aide is making arrangements for Dan's burial in Biloxi."

"What a shock. Three nights ago, Dan and Remy came to my apartment for dinner to celebrate Dan's sixtieth birthday."

Angela shook her head. "It was so sudden. Not many women wake up in the middle of the night and find a corpse."

During the afternoon, the admiral's aide had arranged for a viewing Saturday evening at the funeral home on Gentilly Boulevard and a memorial service Sunday morning. As a retired Air Force officer, Dan was entitled to be buried in the National Cemetery in Biloxi, Mississippi. Meanwhile, Ellen began planning food for the wake after the burial. She made a list of what each woman would cook and asked the men to supply beer and liquor.

Angela spent the night again so Remy wouldn't be alone. I promised to be there early Saturday morning to help anyway I could. When I arrived in the morning, Vince came to pick up Angela so she could change clothes before returning that afternoon for the viewing.

"How can I help?" I asked.

Remy, true to her years as a military wife, insisted that the apartment be spotless when Jacquie, Dan's brothers, and friends came back from the cemetery Sunday.

"Dan always vacuumed the house, did the laundry, and washed the windows for me," said Remy. "Guess I'll have to learn to do those things for myself from now on."

I vacuumed and dusted the two-bedroom apartment, which

was no quick or easy job because of Remy's collection of figurines and music boxes.

Even though the rain continued to pour down in buckets, Remy insisted on washing windows, inside and out. I looked through a window at Remy, who was standing outside on the soggy lawn scrubbing the glass. The rain beat horizontally on the window as Remy tried to dry it. Her hair was matted from the rain, and her face was streaked with tears mixed with rain. Ah well, I thought, keeping busy was the best outlet for grief.

A few of our coworkers returned in the early afternoon and brought sandwiches and salads. While Remy dried her hair and dressed for the evening's viewing hours, the admiral's aide went to the airport to pick up Remy's daughter, who had flown in from California. She was Remy's daughter from her first marriage, and she lived in Los Angeles with her Latino husband and their two children.

Remy's first husband and his wife also arrived. Jacquie had called her father to tell him about Dan's funeral. Remy and Jacquie's father had remained friends after their divorce and their remarriages.

Dan's two brothers, one younger than Dan and one older, and their wives arrived from Illinois in time for the viewing. They were tall, handsome men like Dan.

Just as everyone was about to leave for the evening memorial service, Remy turned to Jacquie. "I forget. I haven't told Mother. I usually call her every Saturday afternoon."

"It's okay, Mom." Jacquie hugged Remy. "I'll tell grandma about Dan. I haven't called her in months."

"Remy, you'd better put on some lipstick. Pink would be perfect," said Angela, handing Remy a small mirror.

"Why are you talking about lipstick? My husband is dead."

"You're white as a virgin princess. Just a touch."

Remy drew faint strokes of color on her wan lips. She stared with filmy eyes at her reflection in the mirror.

"You make a gorgeous widow," Angela said.

The Santorinis drove Remy and Jacquie to the viewing. I rode with Ellen and Alex.

Flowers filled the funeral home. Dazzling sprays of roses, lilies, and gladiolas with white ribbons, some embossed with Dan's name, and bows and wreaths on wire legs were nestled among curly-legged chairs and corners of the room. Little wire trees sprouting red and pink roses amid spikes of shivering ferns stood in nooks around the room. Sprinkled with glistening droplets of water, the bouquets' sweet perfume hung in the air.

Friends arrived, signed the guest register, and hugged Remy. She received their awkward sympathies and strange smiles gracefully. Dark-suited guests tiptoed to the coffin for one last look at Dan, resting serenely handsome on a blue satin comforter.

By nine p.m., everyone had left. Jacquie and Remy rode home with Vince and Angela. Ellen and Alex dropped me off in front of my apartment building.

Before the memorial service Sunday morning, friends brought more food to Remy's. I added my platter of deviled eggs to the dining room table laden with plates of ham, turkey, gumbo, red beans and rice, jambalaya, cold cuts, French bread, and whiskey bread pudding. It's what people do. They don't know what else to do, so they bring food. It's the custom. A few women stayed in the apartment to spread out the feast for the mourners and to mind the children.

The rain wasn't about to let up just because it was Sunday morning and time for Dan's funeral. I rode with Ellen and Alex to the 9 a.m. service.

The chilly funeral parlor smelled like a florist shop's refrigerator. More flower arrangements had arrived from family friends and out-of-state relatives, including Remy's mother.

"Thank you for coming." Ellen and Dan's sisters-in-law greeted guests entering the room. "Please sign the register."

"Poor Remy. Such a shock." The women glanced at Remy, who was wearing a black dress that she kept for special occasions.

She sat between Jacquie and one of Dan's brothers on a long sofa in front of the casket.

People gathered in groups around the room. Soon, others walked between the rows of metal chairs to the recessed niche where the gleaming brass and dark wood casket lay. More flowers and a crucifix on a mahogany stand had been placed behind the hexagonal casket, and at each end candles flickered in tall, red glass holders.

An Episcopal priest began the liturgy and led the group in prayer. A recorded "Ava Maria" played softly in the background. The priest said something that made everyone think he knew Dan, but as far as I knew, he had never met Dan. The reverend lamented Dan's untimely death, his being struck down in the prime of life, leaving behind a beautiful, loving wife and grieving brothers.

When Remy walked to the casket and bent over to kiss Dan, she moved as if something inside her was broken.

After the service, people piled into cars and followed the hearse. Remy and Jacquie rode with Vince and Angela, and I rode with the O'Reillys. The caravan traveled east along I-10 to Biloxi, about 80 miles from New Orleans.

"Will the rain ever stop?" I asked as Alex drove silently.

In the midst of the downpour, hail pounded the car and tried to drill holes through its steel roof. Wave after wave of rain washed over the Gulf coast road, as the wind rushed through sycamores and cypresses, bending and twisting the branches, tearing leaves and limbs from trees. In the distance we heard thunder boomers and saw lightning strikes that lit up the gray sky. The National Cemetery was located adjacent to Keesler Air Force Base in Biloxi, Mississippi.

Some thirty of Dan's friends, including the Facility's admirals, retired Air Force friends from Florida, and members of Rex Rampart's band had gathered around the flagpole in the center of the cement circle at one end of the cemetery.

I joined the women huddled under umbrellas, as the rain pocked the cement, splashed upward, and drenched their shoes and stockings. The men had gathered in a group nearby. With a reporter's ear for eavesdropping, I heard the men talking about Dan.

"I haven't seen Dan since he attended my daughter's christening. He was her godfather," said one of Dan's brothers. "He was always the healthy one in the family. I never thought he'd be the first to go."

"I can't believe it," said Dan's younger brother.

"Glenda and I first met Dan in Budapest," said Hank Smith. "After he and his first wife broke up, I didn't think he'd ever remarry. They had married right after high school, and the young bride couldn't take the separation that Air Force life brings. She started running around with airmen while Dan was away. He got a divorce quickly and seemed to enjoy his bachelor life until he met Remy."

"Dan was one of my best friends," said Vince. "When Angela and I applied for a bank loan to buy our bar, Dan co-signed for us. We paid off the loan years before we quit the business. Luckily, Dan didn't have to come up with the money, but I know he'd have kept his promise. That's how he is, er..., was."

Bruno, Rex's pianist, agreed. "Dan was everyone's friend. I'll never forget the many evenings I spent with Dan and Remy. I'd pick up Kentucky Fried Chicken on the way to their apartment and we'd play poker all night. Dan usually won the pot, but he always let me win back some chips."

"Ladies and gentlemen, if everyone's here, let's gather around." The Air Force chaplain began reading the Twenty-third Psalm. Later, as he offered a few prayers, sorrow washed over the friends like a black flood. Savagely, the rain attacked as though the death of Dan was not grief enough for one day.

Then we walked a short distance to the gravesite, where the casket was sitting atop a metal stand. Except for the road, the entire field of gravestones was inundated with water and appeared to sink deeper into the mud with each drop of rain.

We gathered around the casket, which looked so small. On

top lay a sodden drape of black silk and a spray of rain-beaded yellow roses. Everyone was quiet; no one moved. The heavens wept for Dan.

Remy's legs buckled under her and she sobbed. Dan's two brothers held her up.

But Dan couldn't be buried, not yet. The mourners wouldn't be able to toss earth on the coffin as it sank below the surface. The gravesite was as full of water as a Jacuzzi. The coffin would have to rest on the stand a few days until the water level subsided. Then, when the ground dried out, hopefully in a day or two, cemetery personnel would bury Dan. He would make his final descent alone.

Remy sobbed aloud. Ellen and Angela cried openly, and I dabbed at the tears filling my eyes and spilling down my cheeks. Remy bent down to kiss the coffin, then turned around silently. She was so pale I thought she might faint if someone didn't get her into a car and back home soon.

We turned, leaving Dan's open grave behind us. Color Dan gone.

The rain subsided slightly as people piled into their cars. Some drove to Florida and others returned to New Orleans. The overcast sky brightened and rays of sunlight threaded through the opening in the clouds, dropping shafts of warm light over the highway. The coastal waves had receded and the wind had slowed down, but the rain trickled on for hours.

New Orleans' jazz funerals, held for musicians and dignitaries, are unique. The marchers start off slowly, shuffling to mournful music. Then after a few respectful minutes, they burst into happy tunes and dance jigs to send the deceased off to heaven. Dan's wake was no less melancholy and no less raucous than a jazz funeral.

Many people returned to Remy's apartment after the funeral. There were Navy couples, a few of Dan's Black friends, including the parking lot attendant Dan always left his car with in the Quarter. Rex Rampart and a few members of the band came in, paid respects to Remy, and left, except for Bruno.

The rooms were crammed, elbow to elbow, cheek to cheek with mourners. Some of the people came because it was their place, but some came to congratulate themselves on being alive. Perhaps people tried to convince themselves they're still alive and healthy, and death was unthinkable. They bemoaned the fact that Dan had "gone south," as the Cajuns say.

Everyone was hungry. It had been an exhausting, emotional day. Coffee and tea were offered, but almost everyone wanted something hard. As usual, Vince bartended.

People were gorging themselves and drinking too much, as if they were afraid they might never eat or drink again. They carried full plates and ate standing up or walking around the room because there were too few chairs. Some people sat on arms of chairs, others stood around the piano or gathered in the kitchen.

To eat food at a time like this, I thought, seemed a betrayal of the deceased, but Dan loved to eat and drink. Everyone, even Remy, appeared to want, and perhaps need, sustenance. We all wanted to be fed. It seemed unsuitable to me, like wanting sex at a time like this. But sorrow still needed to be fed, and Remy was dealing with her disconsolate emptiness by feeding everyone who gathered around her to offer their support. Every time Dan's name was mentioned, Remy grimaced and tried to hold back her tears. His name was a land mine for her.

Friends paid their respects to Remy and then met in the corners of the room to talk about the affairs of life. People talked cheerfully, as New Orleans people do after a death, as if it was what the dead person wanted. People were drinking plenty. They talked freely, loudly, as if it would be an insult to whisper like they do up North. They told stories and laughed because that's what Dan would have wanted and that's how he lived his life—heavy drinking, eating, joking.

After eating a small plateful of ham and salad, I perched on a stool between Angela and Ellen and leaned an elbow on the padded bar around the piano.

"You must be tired, Ellen. You did a good job organizing

everything."

"Thanks. I didn't mind. I like to make sure everything is in order."

"Yes, I can see that. I don't know what the Facility would do without you. You'd better not retire too soon. You know, I've never been to such a joyous funeral," I said.

"We celebrate our loved ones away," said Angela, "to the other side."

"I guess wakes are more for the living than the deceased."

"Yeah. The dead couldn't care less," she chortled.

Bruno was playing the piano and sipping whiskey and sodas. Gold chains dripped down his open shirt and disappeared into his hairy chest. You couldn't hear much of the music over the din of people chattering, repeating and laughing at Dan's old jokes, trying to cheer up one another.

"Anyone who doesn't think the death toll is high should see the funeral director's bill," someone's voice carried over the din.

"Yeah. With the high cost of doctors and funerals, we can't afford to live or die."

The apartment became stuffy from warm bodies, as well as cigar and cigarette smoke. When I opened a livingroom window, the wind and rain blew inside. The Venetian blinds clickety-clacked like an accountant using an abacus.

After a while, someone put on some tapes. Happy songs that made everyone sad, remembering how Dan celebrated life. He wouldn't hear those songs again; wouldn't ramble and wouldn't march. The music celebrated the release of his soul.

As the noise became louder and louder, Alex turned to the people sitting around him. "This reminds me of an old Irish saying: the sleep that knows no waking is always followed by a wake that knows no sleeping."

Everyone laughed. Jokes relieved the tension everyone felt. Dan was being resurrected in the hearts and memories of those who loved him. The nearness of death frightened them, but its presence made them laugh.

"Oooh. This is a wake, you're supposed to be serious."

"Not if you're Irish." Alex relit his pipe. "The Gaels in Ireland have a custom. They laugh at death and usually make love in the fields outside on the night of a wake to defy death."

I smiled. But, of course, this wasn't an Irish wake.

Over the din of laughter and talking, I heard someone, who was well into his cups, shout, "Only the young die good."

"You mean, only the good die young," someone answered.

"Well, a man's dying is more the survivors' affair than his own."

During early evening, the phone rang. One of Dan's brothers answered it. "Jacquie, it's your husband."

She went into the bedroom to speak to him because she couldn't hear him over the funereal hubbub in the livingroom. When Jacquie returned from the bedroom, she hugged Remy.

"What's wrong, honey?"

Tearfully, Jacquie said, "He wants me to come home tomorrow. He said he could hear all the noise going on here; a party he called it. He said evidently I wasn't needed."

"A penny for your thoughts," Ellen turned to me.

"I was remembering my father's funeral. I was twelve. After the burial, all the relatives and friends returned to our house in Riverdale, Maryland. The relatives needed food to nourish them before they drove the three or four hours back to Philadelphia. When they left, Mother and I felt bereaved, just like Remy does now. Even though my father had been sick for a year, his death was still a shock. Dan's death was so sudden. He was the nicest man I've ever met."

"Yes, Dan was good, honest, reliable, gentle, even sweet. Everyone he came in contact with liked him," said Ellen, wiping a graying blonde hair from her forehead. "He had his basket of trips."

"Death makes all men perfect," cackled Angela, who was feeling the effects of too many bourbons. "He made a handsome corpse."

"Oooh."

I snickered. "Please. Let's have some respect for the dead."

Remy, carrying a plate of salad and cold cuts, came over to the piano. She put her plate on the bar and stretched her arms across our shoulders. I was amazed the way Remy appeared to keep moving past her shock and the grief, past the hollowness she must feel inside.

Alex asked Bruno to play "Danny Boy." When he began playing, people gathered around the piano to sing. Vince's rich tenor voice prevailed above the others. Tears came to everyone's eyes and Remy sobbed. Somehow, we finished singing the song. A tribute to Dan.

"There's a new star in heaven tonight, Remy," said Ellen.

"Dan's epitaph should read: Here lies one of those rare souls who will enrich heaven," I added.

About the time Dan's wake threatened to turn into a bacchanal, the well-wishers began drifting out to their cars. Around midnight, all the kisses, waves, hugs, and tears were over.

When the apartment was empty, Jacquie and I cleaned up the livingroom and kitchen. Women had brought more than enough food, so I sorted through the dishes, deciding what to refrigerate and what to freeze.

Before she began emptying ashtrays, Remy put on a tape, "A Closer Walk." She was smiling.

"What are you smiling about?" Jacquie asked her mother.

"I was just thinking. Dan is happy. Back to the earth, dust to dust." She hummed with the music and picked up Pooh. "Listen to this music. Could music in heaven be any better than this?"

She lifted Pooh high above her head. They began turning, dancing to the rhythm. She held the cat's right paw in one hand, and nuzzled her white cheek to the beat of the music.

"Onetwothreefour, onetwothreefour," Remy crooned as the slow jazzy, melancholy foxtrot reached its full sadness. Remy and Pooh danced round and round, circling among the chairs. Remy kissed Pooh's cheek and set her down on Dan's chair.

"Dear God, help me." Remy stretched her arms heavenward. There was pain in her eyes. She slumped onto the sofa, buried her head in her arms, and sobbed. "How can I find the courage to get out of bed in the morning? I can't imagine surviving another day like this one. This emptiness is going to kill me." She drew in her breath sharply and tilted her head back and shut her eyes. She must be seeing Dan, I thought.

Jacquie put her arms around her mother's shoulders. "Dan would want you to finish the course, Mother, not give up. No matter how long and hard and lonely the way. You know that. You have to put one foot in front of the other."

I felt Remy's sorrow. I knew what it was to grieve for a dead father, a dead sister, if not a husband. I had faced the abyss of separation, colder than an arctic plain, wider than any sea, deeper than a pit in hell.

When Remy stopped shaking, Jacquie led her into the bedroom. Dan was dead. Not all Remy's tears or all her wishes would change that reality.

I left the apartment and walked around the lake to my building. I felt like I was walking through a graveyard at midnight.

Sometimes, life turns you inside out. The one thing you can count on is surprise. For Remy, life wasn't about to just turn her inside out, it was soon to toss her upside down, around, and then right side up.

CHAPTER FOUR

The amazing thing about another person's death is that life goes on. The hole gets filled up slowly, just like the grave, until the ground is level again, smoothed flat. Memory grows like grass over the remains. After the funeral, life begins to rearrange, and time promises to pass much as it always has.

On a Sunday evening two weeks after Dan Rawley's funeral, Remy invited me to her apartment for happy hour. She was stirring a pitcher of martinis when I arrived. We sat in the livingroom and listened to a Pete Fountain tape.

"A martini is instant bliss, isn't it?"

"Amen." Remy sipped her drink. "It's *the* drink for attitude-adjustment time. It gives me a sense of peace and a pleasant tingling from head to toe."

"Wasn't it Marlene Dietrich who said that one martini was okay, two made her buzz, three put her under the table, and after four, she was under the host."

Remy laughed.

"Has Jacquie gone home?"

"Yes. Tuesday."

"Did she have to go back so soon?"

"Her husband demanded it, that's why," said Remy. "When he called Sunday evening, he heard everyone talking and laughing in the background. He figured we were having too much fun and Jacquie wasn't needed here."

"Not very sympathetic, eh? Guess he doesn't understand the New Orleans' *joie de vivre.*"

"He's a Spic chauvinist pig."

"That's a rough way to talk about him." I was a little surprised when Remy called her son-in-law a Spic. She didn't say it in a nasty way, but I attributed her use of this derogatory term for Mexicans and Puerto Ricans to her upbringing in the bowels of New York City. My years as a journalist in the Pacific had certainly made me color-blind and culture-blind. I took everyone at face value, according to their actions. *Viva la difference*, I always say.

Remy sniffed. "He rules the house. I think he slaps Jacquie around, but she's afraid to leave him. She says she still loves him. He *is* a handsome devil. If it weren't for my adorable granddaughters, I'd never go visit that family. I'd let Jacquie come here to see me. I miss her."

"She looks a lot like you."

"Actually, she looks more like her father."

"What's he like?"

"Oh, he's a good, decent man, an expert accountant. But husband? Everything in moderation is his motto. He's dull, a bore, with no imagination. Sex was dull. I became indifferent to him."

I nodded. "Indifference can kill a marriage, that's for sure."

"I never thought of leaving him until I met Dan. I had never been unfaithful before. Although I admit I had some offers, I didn't follow through."

We were silent for a few minutes, drinking in the soothing sounds of Pete Fountain's smooth clarinet.

"Was Jacquie an only child?" I asked.

Remy nodded. "So was I."

"Me, too. You know people say that only children are spoiled, selfish. But I don't think you or I turned out so bad, did we?"

"No. Neither did Jacquie. You know, I'm tired of rattling around this apartment alone. If I didn't have Pooh, I don't know what I'd do. She misses Dan, too."

"Have you eaten yet?"

Remy shook her head.

"Let's go to the Peking Restaurant across the street. My treat," I said.

We lingered over a delicious dinner of whole steamed fish with rice and vegetables.

"I blame myself for Dan's death," said Remy. "His cholesterol was too high, and his blood pressure too. I should have watched his diet. Too many martinis and Kentucky Fried Chicken. Guess those occasional cigars didn't help either. But, you know, he was never sick. No colds, no headaches."

"Don't blame yourself. I understand your grief. You don't have to talk about it."

"I need to. Dan was such a wonderful, loving man. I wish I had died instead of him."

"Don't say that. None of us is ever prepared for the loss of a loved one," said Grace. "Nothing softens the loss."

"One day I was Mrs. Dan Rawley. Today, I'm a widow."

When we paid the bill, the owner returned our receipt with two Chinese fortune cookies.

I broke open my cookie. 'Love never runs smoothly', it says. Ha, that I found out the hard way a long time ago."

"Oh, my God." Remy handed her fortune to me.

'If you let it, adversity will enfold you like mold,' I read. "This doesn't mean a Chinese tinkily-dink."

After dinner, we returned to Remy's apartment for a nightcap. Remy put on a tape, "Help Me Make It Through the Night."

"I feel like a two-ton weight has fallen on my chest and crushed it. It never once occurred to me that one day Dan wouldn't be here. I wake up missing him like sin. He was my anchor, my armor against the world."

I thought Remy was completely drained by Dan's death. "Cherish those twenty happy years you and Dan had. They're memories now, but Dan will live forever deep in your heart."

"Yeah. In my broken heart." Remy sobbed and buried her face in her hands. "Do you think it's easy to forget?"

"I didn't say it was easy. You don't have to forget those precious memories."

"You're alone. You don't know what it is to fall asleep at night in the arms of the one you love. I think of his kisses, and his hand touching mine, and his looks of love. If I don't have Dan, I don't want to go on living. I wish God had taken me too. What on earth do I have to live for now?"

"You're an intelligent woman. Your friends need you. Your daughter and grandchildren need you. The admirals need you. Speaking of work, have you thought about returning to work?"

"I haven't given it much thought. But maybe I should go back tomorrow. I can't rattle around here forever." She stood, picked up Pooh from Dan's chair, and kissed her. "She's been sleeping there since Dan died."

We were silent for a few minutes, then Remy started to titter to herself.

"What's so funny?"

"I was thinking about the wake," she blushed. "In the middle of the evening, I felt like I wanted to have sex. It was overpowering."

"Well, didn't Alex say that in Ireland people always have sex after a wake? Maybe Mother Nature was trying to tell you something."

"Could be. During our years together, Dan satisfied my needs, my desires. He overlooked, even joked, about my flirting with his male friends because he knew that my heart belonged to him. He fulfilled all my fantasies." She became quiet, a secret smile radiating across her face.

The week after Dan's funeral, the admiral's aide had collected Dan's clothing to take to the Salvation Army. But a few days later, Remy said she found a pair of Dan's trousers hanging on a hook in the closet.

"I took the pants down from the hook and pressed them to my face and cried," she said. "Then I heard change jingling. In the back pocket I found five quarters, a clip of dollar bills, and a wad of papers, slightly wrinkled, curved from having been sat on. There was a receipt from Albertson's for a package of lightbulbs, a loaf of French bread, a half-dozen oranges, and fifths of vodka and scotch. There was a shopping list. Every morning Dan made a 'to do' list. This one was typical: restoration committee meeting 10 a.m., Albertsons, brother's birthday, meet Herb for lunch, make reservations at Gallatoires for Remy's birthday dinner."

Remy got up and changed the tape on the recorder. "Why don't you ride with me to work tomorrow instead of taking the bus?"

"Are you sure you want to go back? It's only been two weeks."

"Yes. I have to do something. Sitting around here watching Pooh mourn in Dan's empty chair makes me break down again. Pooh hardly leaves his chair except to eat. Occasionally she sits on my lap and lets me pet her. "

"I'd love to ride with you. I can sleep an extra hour in the morning." I was thrilled at the thought of a twenty-minute ride to work instead of the hour and a half by bus.

"Wish I could do that," said Remy.

"Why can't you?"

"I get up every morning at four to wash my hair. It takes me an hour to blow-dry and style it. Speaking of hair, Dan used to color my hair. Now I'll have to get it dyed at the beauty shop where I get my nails done each month."

"I don't see how you can type with those inch-long nails."

Remy looked at her perfectly manicured nails that complemented her long, graceful hands. "They don't bother me. They're acrylic. They don't break easily."

Remy was always neatly groomed and freshly clothed. Not everyone would call her beautiful: maybe too tall, too regal, too stiff. But men seldom realized it when caught by her charm. When she flirted with men through those golden-flecked eyes and that mischievous twinkle, she owned them body and soul. She wore her femininity like an expensive perfume.

"Ever since I started working at the Facility, I've wondered how the Navy Facility came to have such elaborate headquarters,"

I said. "I've never worked in such a fancy government building, especially in what I presume was once a riverfront warehouse." The Facility had a squash court, a commissary, a post office, and a cafeteria on the ground level and five floors of employee parking and offices, including Chiefs' and Officers' Clubs.

"You're right. When an admiral retired from active duty, he was elected to the U.S. Senate. It didn't hurt that he was the son of an influential and wealthy N'awlins family. After his term in Washington, the admiral agreed to return to active duty if he could head the Navy Facility in his home town. Congress gave him the go-ahead and unlimited funds to renovate the warehouse. He was head of the Facility for ten years before he retired the second time."

"That's some story."

"Did you notice he had a private elevator installed to take him from his first-floor parking space to his sixth floor office?"

I nodded. "Isn't it amazing what a family name and Congressional clout can do?"

Remy laughed. "I forgot to tell you. Vince helped me sell our two cars. They were both five years old, so I traded them in for a new Buick Regal. I'll pick it up soon."

"Sounds like a good deal."

"I don't know what I'd have done without Angela and Vince. They helped me so much after Dan died. Vince, especially. He's so sweet and caring."

Three days later, Remy and I went to work in her new emerald-colored two-door Buick.

"I love the smell of a new car, don't you?"

Remy snorted. "Someone else likes new cars too."

"What do you mean?"

"My hubcaps were stolen last night," Remy said as she braked at the railroad tracks to wait for a freight train to pass.

"Gosh, I didn't notice."

"It's disgusting. The first night the car's off the sales lot, the hubcaps are ripped off. Probably taken by one of our nigger neighbors to sell to buy drugs."

Again, I was surprised at Remy's language, but then I thought, perhaps there was a side of her that I didn't quite know. "You should file an insurance claim."

"I intend to. Then I'll buy some cheap hubcaps that no one would want to steal. This apartment complex has really gone downhill since Dan and I first moved in."

"I passed by the swimming pool on the way over here," I said. "It looks like someone had an all-night orgy and tossed the pool furniture into the water. They sure ruin life for everyone, not to mention destroying Kenilworth's pool and furniture."

We drove down Chef Menteur highway. As we neared the bridge over the Industrial Canal, I said to Remy, "You can't imagine how wonderful it is not to have to ride the bus or, especially, how nice it is to ride with a sane driver instead of Betty."

"Betty?"

"You know, the accountant who also lives at Kenilworth. She drove me out to see the Kenilworth manager one evening when I was apartment hunting."

"Oh, yeah. You think she's crazy?"

"Sort of. She scared me to death twice. That's why I stopped riding with her and chose to suffer miserable bus rides ever since."

"What happened?"

"One morning as we were approaching the drawbridge across the Industrial Canal, I heard the bells ringing to warn us that the bridge was rising to let a shrimp boat pass below. I yelled at Betty. She's hard of hearing, you know. She ignored me. She kept on going—we made it across the bridge just as it was beginning to rise."

"Good heavens. No wonder you were scared."

"That's not all. One day as we were about to cross the railroad tracks farther into town, the red light on the wooden gate was flashing and it was coming down. Betty, running late as usual, rammed the gate, breaking off a foot or so of it, and we sped across the tracks."

"Fortunately, you made it."

"By the skin of our teeth. She's a terrible driver."

"Well, let's hope we don't have any of those episodes. I'll be careful. I enjoy your company. It makes the drive seem shorter."

"Thanks. I appreciate riding with you."

Remy was the sister I never had. I think I filled Remy's need for a sister, a confidante, too. Remy's new role as a widow put her, unwillingly, into a different lifestyle than her married friends, Ellen and Angela.

After a steamy summer, a chilly autumn zoomed in on the Crescent City. The city seemed to settle closer to the damp earth, and the fall hurricane season was warming up in the Gulf of Mexico. The sky was often brilliant blue with clean white clouds blowing from the river, letting through the weak sun to warm the spirit. The frosty air didn't seem to ease Remy's pain. I thought she was like a dormant volcano about to erupt.

One Sunday Angela invited me to come with Remy to brunch on the West Bank. The Rawleys and Santorinis had been doing this for at least ten years, like a weekly family ritual. Vince and Angela went to early Mass each Sunday, then they'd wait for Dan and Remy to arrive. Angela said the brunches were modern versions of Italians' old eat-'til-you-bust Sunday get-togethers.

Remy and I arrived at the Santorinis' house around 11 a.m. They lived in a double shotgun house, which reminded me of the row houses in Baltimore or Philadelphia, except those were usually three-story brick structures. Wooden shotguns, also connected in a row, had a tunnel-like foyer barely wide enough for three people to stand. A narrow hallway led from the livingroom to the bedroom, to a dining room, past a bath, to the kitchen. The back door opened onto a small porch and fenced-in yard. The word "shotgun" came from the saying that you could fire a shotgun from the foyer and the bullet would make a beeline to the back door. When their family grew, the Santorinis bought the house next door. They had an archway cut in the center wall leading into the other shotgun, which they converted into spacious bedrooms for their four children.

Angela hugged Remy and me. Vince gave me a quick hug, then held Remy in his arms for a few minutes.

"Vince, why don't you make us some drinks?" Angela said abruptly.

Vince seemed reluctant to let Remy go, but, obeying his wife, he went to the dining room liquor cabinet to mix dry vodka martinis. He put ice cubes in a tall glass pitcher, poured in four parts Smirnoff vodka and slightly less than one part Noilly Prat Vermouth, then stirred for 10 seconds. He removed the ice cubes and swizzled the martinis a few more seconds, added a slice of lime peel, and let the mixture rest. He poured the drinks through a strainer into four old-fashioned glasses, then stuck an olive and an onion on a toothpick in each drink.

"Hmm, this is perfect." I took a sip. "It's so icy, refreshing, like skinny-dipping in an arctic pool."

Vince winked.

Vince's rigid posture made him appear taller than he was. To offset his five-foot-six frame, he wore custom-made shoes with one-and-one-half-inch lifts. I thought Vince had a certain something, I couldn't quite put my finger on, that exuded sex. Always a sharp dresser, he was smooth and his dark looks drew women's attention. His mouth was full and erotic, with lips women longed to touch. Women melted in the dark brown laser beam of his steady gaze. Virility was like a gloss all over him.

For his job as bartender at Rex's club, he wore a bow tie, a red vest, and a pseudo-tuxedo black jacket and pants. The collar and cuffs of his starched white shirt were so stiff that a tennis ball would have bounced off them. The red carnation in his lapel buttonhole was always fresh. His black shoes were spit-polished. Vince wasn't only the singing bartender at the club. He acted as a bodyguard, keeping the public, especially ga-ga women, away from the musicians.

Vince and Angela didn't think of themselves as Italians or Italian Americans, more like New Orleanians. They were born in New Orleans. Their parents were born in Sicily.

Vince was a descendant of the Mafia, that invisible army of soldiers who had been prominent in New Orleans for four decades. In the 1890s, large sections of New Orleans were settled by Italian immigrants, some of whom were offsprings of Sicilian Mafia.

When we finished our drinks, we piled into Vince's big hearse-black Oldsmobile sedan for the trip across the river.

Vince took the long way through New Orleans. We drove down Elysian Fields, which runs between the railroad tracks and the river. This section is poor, but has a raffish charm. The houses are mainly white frame, weathered grey, with rickety, faded white outside stairs and galleries, and quaintly ornamented gables.

Vince drove slowly so I could savor the charm of the quarter. I could tell how close to his heart the scenes around us were. He spoke with pride about his city.

On Chartres Street in the Quarter, we passed prostitutes sitting, legs akimbo, on the stoops of their row houses, while others leaned out from upstairs windows and waved at passing cars.

"Those women look like they just woke up," I said.

"Never on Sundays, eh?" quipped Remy.

"Guess they ply their trade six days a week," said Vince. "If they make money on Sundays, their pimps cheer."

"They look so sad and worn out," I said.

"Do you know how red-light districts got that name?" asked Angela.

I nodded.

"Narrow, paintless houses, called cribs, sat in rows like bad teeth near the railroad tracks. In the nineteenth century, trainmen would leave their red lanterns outside saloons or cribs. That way, bosses could round up their men when the train was ready to leave."

As we drove across the bridge to the West Bank, Angela said, "Some people think the West Bank is foreign country. They wouldn't cross the bridge if their life depended on it. Even tourists rarely see what's on the other side of the Mississippi."

"Why?" I asked.

"Well, it is like another country. More downhome, unsophisticated, rundown in some parts. There're several housing projects over here, too."

We drove along the West Bank Expressway, passing small seedy towns. There were low, dilapidated buildings, dingy nightclubs, hamburger stands, and gun shops. More often than not, Confederate flags hung in the doorways, and morose country songs blasted from jukeboxes. We passed a Black housing project, placed cheek by jowl with blue-collar whites in mobile homes, and little lanes lined with neat, prefab bungalows with iron bars on every window.

Each Sunday, the two couples usually went to the same restaurant built on a pier over the Mississippi in Marrero. Though they tried new places now and then, they always came back to this restaurant.

Inside, where dozens of mounted fish decorated the walls, the spicy aromas of filé and cayenne pepper permeated the air. At the table, I scanned the foot-high menu. It offered Cajun specialties of blackened catfish, gumbo, boudin, jambalaya, shrimp, and crawfish. Other dishes were veal piccata, cooked in wine, butter and laced with crawfish tails and shitake mushrooms sauteed in roasted garlic, capers, and herb beurre blanc; filet mignon surrounded by French mushrooms sauteed in roasted garlic on Cajun potato hay and laced with Creolaise sauce; black truffle slices sauteed in champagne and herb butter sauce with lobster claw meat on garlic croutons; alligator medallions with Dijon mustard sauce; crawfish spring rolls with ginger and beurre blanc; and crawfish Caesar salad. Desserts included bananas Foster, cheesecake, and pecan pie.

Vince ordered his favorite appetizers: a plate of deep fried calamari and alligator bits.

"Do you like calamari? It's squid, you know. We can get something else if you'd like," Angela told me.

"I've never had it, but I'd like to try it. I haven't tried alligator either."

When the plates arrived, I bit into a piece of calamari. "Mm-mm. Delicious." It was crisp, almost voluptuous.

The waiter took our orders: I wanted to try the crawfish spring rolls, Remy ordered blackened catfish, Angela opted for veal piccata, and Vince selected the filet mignon. Of course, we all had vodka martinis before, during, and after dinner.

"Does every dish in New Orleans contain garlic?" I asked.

Angela laughed. "Just about. Garlic is called Cajun perfume, or sometimes Italian perfume. Our motto is 'in garlic we trust.'"

I giggled so hard I almost choked on a calamari leg.

"Are you all right?"

I nodded. I could feel my face turning red.

"Never laugh when you eat shrimp, or oysters, for that matter. I had a friend who died on his wedding day. He laughed and choked to death while chewing on a shrimp," said Vince.

When I recovered, I said, "Remy tells me you two used to own a bar in the Quarter."

"Yes." Angela put down her fork and sighed. "Soon after we were married, 40 years ago, we opened Evangeline's Desire Bar, just a block off Bourbon Street. Vince and I both tended bar. I cooked gumbo, jambalaya, and red beans and rice. We always served free snacks to customers and had a jazz combo on weekends. Maybe that's why we went broke, but at least we still had each other. That's when Vince went to work for Rex Rampart."

"Evangeline's quite a common name around here, I've noticed."

"Yea. There are Evangeline race tracks, bars, speedways, drive-ins, whorehouses, and even Evangeline Maid bread," said Vince, slicing off a piece of filet.

"Didn't Longfellow's poem *Evangeline* relate to this area?"

"Yes," said Angela. "It's based on a true story about the Acadians' troubled journey to Louisiana in the 1600s. These people migrated from France to Acadie, now Nova Scotia, when the British threw them out of Canada. Some came to Louisiana territory, ruled by Spain then.

"As the poem goes, young Evangeline was separated from her fiancé, Gabriel, during the migration. She searched for him for years. By the time they were reunited, Evangeline had become a nun, and Gabriel was dying of the plague. Evangeline died of a broken heart while sitting beneath an oak in St. Martinville.

"The true story is that Emmeline Labiche and her fiancé, Louis Arceneaux, were placed on separate ships during the exile and both made their way to Louisiana. Louis landed in St. Martinville, and a year later, Emmeline arrived, still toting her wedding gown. There she learned of Louis' marriage to another woman. Heartbroken, Emmeline died a few months later. Emmeline's grave is located behind St. Martin's de Tour Catholic Church, the mother church of the Acadians. The couple's romance, as well as Acadian life, are kept alive in the Longfellow-Evangeline State Commemorative Area outside St. Martinville. The story would have died, except for Longfellow's poem."

"What a sad story." I recalled that Oscar Wilde once said, "Those who are faithless know the pleasures of love; it is the faithful who know love's tragedies." This reminded me of Remy. She and Dan had such an ideal marriage, but it ended too soon. Still, she was lucky to have had twenty years with him.

On the way back to New Orleans after lunch, I asked, "What's the difference between Cajun and Creole cooking?"

"Cajuns eat anything that doesn't eat them first," said Vince.

Angela cackled. "Well, the lines are blurred between Cajun and Creole cooking these days. A pure Cajun gumbo begins with a dark brown roux with a pork or chicken stock and Andouille sausage. A Creole gumbo contains tomatoes and more of a variety of ingredients. But every cook has her own way of doing things. There are many varieties of gumbo. When my sister and I make gumbo, you wouldn't think they were the same dish."

"Just like the various recipes for Swiss muesli," I said.

"The practice of cooking with tomatoes and hot peppers, as in jambalaya and gumbo, came from Spain and the Caribbean. Here, gumbo is eaten with rice, a crop introduced by the French. Typically Cajun is crawfish, sometimes called mudbugs. These are boiled or steamed, and Cajuns suck their heads. Cajun haute cuisine combines simple Cajun country cooking with contemporary ingredients and Creole styles."

Vince said, "It's said that Cajuns don't eat to live, they live to eat."

We all laughed.

"There's always been a thing between the Creoles and Cajuns in Louisiana. Creoles were descendants of Spanish and French nobility, plantation owners whose ancestors had founded New Orleans, with old families like Villeres and Charbonnets. Their families go back five generations on each side and include governors and Spanish territorial officers," Angela explained.

As we drove along the Belle Chasse Highway towards New Orleans, a flock of large blue snipes flew low across the grille of the car and veered into the greenish mist rising above the Mississippi.

Later at Remy's apartment, she told me that Angela was an alcoholic. "She lost her driver's license after an accident. When their bar lost money, maybe due in part to Angela's drinking up all the booze, they sold it. But Angela has a big heart. She's a good Italian wife and a great cook.

"From time to time, Angela gets jealous of Vince. She knows that his voice and his black silky hair that curls over his twinkling brown eyes attracts women. He defends himself, when Angela talks about the women who surround him at the club by saying, can I help it if women can't resist me."

"That's a shame. I think Angela's one of the sweetest women I've ever known." I soon learned that deep beneath her cheery, innocent facade lay a dark soul capable of sinister thoughts and deeds.

CHAPTER FIVE

Early winter was mild, with balmy days. The grass in the fields was soft green and nights were touched with a faint chill. Skies remained porcelain blue, and the leaves of cypress, gum, and willow trees remained on.

In November, Remy and I were eating dinner at the Peking Restaurant when I suggested, "Let's take a trip over Christmas. You shouldn't be alone this year."

Remy's face lit up. "Dan and I had planned to go to London this year...."

"Let's go somewhere new to both of us. Maybe Mexico City. Ever been there?"

"No."

"Neither have I. Tomorrow after work let's go to the travel agent at The Plaza and make reservations. Christmas in Mexico City should be exciting."

Remy agreed. The next evening, the travel agent at the Plaza arranged our trip.

On December 22 after dinner, Remy put Pooh in a cat carrier, and we drove to Bruno's house in Metairie. Bruno, the pianist with Rex Rampart's band who had played piano at Dan's wake, had offered to take care of Pooh for the week.

Metairie, a twenty-minute drive on the expressway from East New Orleans, passed for an uptown suburb. When friends moved there, some locals considered it so far out they kissed them goodbye and practically packed them off with a team of huskies.

But Metairie was about as nonthreatening a neighborhood as existed anywhere. The kind with bikes parked in the driveways and shabby sheep dogs lying on porches. Statues of Virgin Mary and Jesus, spotlighted in house gardens, shone like sentinels of God at night, protecting their owners' lawns and foliage from desecration. On one block, twelve Virgin Marys were outlined in the green glow from neon Dixie beer signs outside nearby bars.

Bruno's house sat just before you crossed the line into Jefferson Parish, in the five-street transition area near the cemeteries, where you had the safety of the suburbs and the social correctness of a New Orleans address.

Welcoming us inside, Bruno hugged Remy and me. Then he made drinks for us and relaxed in a lounge chair. His huge house was furnished with comfortable heirloom sofas and chairs or replicas of antiques from Hurwitz-Mintz. There was a brick fireplace in the livingroom and a bar in the adjoining game room.

He picked up Pooh and stroked her silky white coat as he listened to our plans for the week. "Sounds interesting. Take your mind off things, Remy," he agreed.

"It'll be new to both of us," I said.

"Hate to drink and run, but we have to finish packing and be at the airport early tomorrow morning." Remy hugged Bruno. "Thanks for taking care of Pooh."

"She's in good hands." When Bruno smiled, the smitch of hair under his lower lip spread out across his chin. "Have fun, you two."

"See you in a week." Remy kissed Pooh.

On the drive back to East New Orleans, Remy told me that she and Dan had met Bruno when they were stationed near Budapest, some ten years ago.

Bruno was born into a middle-class family in New Orleans. His father was Negro and his mother was Chocktaw. That accounted for Bruno's black hair, as stiff as steel wool. When he was 15 years old, his parents died, leaving him a small inheritance. He enrolled in city college, but by his sophomore year he dropped out and joined the U.S. Civil Service as a commissary procurer and was transferred to Europe. Meanwhile, he married and bought a house in Metairie. His wife died in a plane crash in Italy. Back in New Orleans, he pursued his dream of playing and composing music.

"That's a cute little goatee or whatever you call it on Bruno's chin."

"Oh, you noticed. It is kind of sexy. Musicians like to wear them. They're called soul patches."

We stopped at the Santorinis to wish them Merry Christmas. Angela called her cousin, a taxi driver, and asked him to drive us to the airport in the morning. She wanted to be sure we had a ride because most cab drivers didn't want to travel to East New Orleans.

After a drink, we went home to finish packing.

At 8 a.m. the next morning, Angela's cousin arrived. On the way to the airport, he promised to pick us up when we returned. Even if we could find a cab at the airport, he said, most drivers didn't want to go to East New Orleans because they would have an empty cab coming back to the city. And some cabbies charged enormous fares to make up the difference.

Remy and I had coffee and a Danish in the airport cafeteria before we caught the 10 a.m. flight.

We landed two hours later at the Mexico City airport. A Sanborn Tour agent met us in the terminal and led us to a van waiting to take us to our hotel.

During the frightening half-hour ride into the city, cars, buses, and trucks were traveling fast, head-on in narrow lanes and all honking their horns. Almost every car wore dents and scratches like war decorations.

"Don't they have traffic rules here?" I asked Remy.

"Sh-h-h. We want to get to the hotel in one piece."

"This traffic is worse than Manila or Bangkok."

Arriving safely, but nervous, Remy and I checked into the Hotel

San Francisco. The hotel was dilapidated but respectable. It sat in the heart of busy downtown Mexico City, within walking distance of the Zocolo, the colonial central plaza. On two nearby main shopping streets, Avenida Cinco de Mayo and Avenido Francisco Madero, were Woolworth's, Sears, Sanborn's, La Ciudad de Mexico, Niza, Palacio de Hierro, and Paris Londres.

Our adjacent rooms were located at the end of a hallway on the third floor. While unpacking, we left our doors open because no one had to pass by our rooms. The rooms were stuffy. The windows didn't open and the air-conditioning wasn't doing much to cool the humid heat. The rooms were sparsely furnished, with a double bed, dresser, chair, and luggage rack. Faded red-patterned curtains hung from the windows and faded red bedspreads lay across the lumpy double beds. The tiny bathrooms were adequate.

After we'd unpacked, we walked to the Latin American Tower. We dodged dogs napping on the sidewalks and small children selling Chiclets. We passed storefronts painted harsh blues and yellows, bright reds and parrot green, gaudy as jungle birds and flowers. Many old-model American cars, which probably had been smuggled across the U.S. border, were parked with two wheels on the sidewalks.

On the 41st floor of the Tower, Remy and I relaxed over Margaritas and soaked up the sockdologer views of the city. Our guidebook was right—this was probably the best view of downtown Mexico City, especially at dusk.

That evening we ate dinner in the Hotel Del Prado's Grille, one of the city's best restaurants.

"I'm starved." Remy studied the menu.

We both ordered Margaritas, tortilla soup, and pepper steak. Mariachis serenaded us while we ate.

Remy cut each piece of steak into little bits, savoring each morsel, as though food was her salvation. I was surprised Remy had such a good appetite. Evidently, grief had nothing to do with her enjoyment of food. Perhaps, I thought, Remy was ready to step back into life again.

On the way back to our hotel around 11 p.m., we walked past scores of families who were strolling in Alameda Park. Parents were buying balloons for their kids and stopping to talk to Santa Claus, who was greeting everyone in the park.

On our first morning in Mexico City, which was Christmas Eve, Remy knocked on the door of my room. When I opened it, Remy waved her hair dryer at me. "I'll never get my hair dry. This thing only runs for three minutes, then shuts off. I have to wait another five minutes before it will run again."

"I thought Mexico had the same voltage as the U.S."

"So did I. It's probably this roach-ridden hotel. Everything works slow here, even the elevator."

"That's why I'd rather walk up and down. I don't trust that relic."

Half an hour later, Remy had managed to dry and style her hair into an acceptable bob. Then we went for a not-too-appetizing breakfast of cold toast and fruit juice at Mannix's Coffee Shop in the Barner Hotel, a block away.

At 9 a.m. our guide, Rudy, picked us up in an air-conditioned limousine for a half-day city tour. We drove through a swanky residential area to the west end of the Paseo de la Reforma, where the Chapaultepec (grasshopper) Castle sits on a landscaped hill surrounded by a park, museums, galleries, concert halls, two lakes, and a zoo. This lovely oasis rose above the stinging brownish smog that tainted the city and residents' lungs.

Rudy followed behind Remy and me as we toured the Palace at the Zocolo, the Metropolitan Cathedral, presidential offices, and the Halls of Montezuma, where many walls were decorated with gigantic murals painted by Diego Rivera, a Mexican artist I learned about in art history classes. I couldn't be sure, but I thought I saw Rudy pinch Remy's derriere every now and then. She ignored him.

Next we went to a government-run handicraft market to look over their products. Remy and I promised each other we'd return here on our own.

Back at the hotel at 3:30, Remy and I ate *comida*, or lunch, in the hotel restaurant.

"Wasn't Rudy cute?"

"If you like short, pudgy Latinos."

"He pinched me when we were walking around the castle."

"I noticed that. I wonder whether he does that to all tall red-heads, eh? Dirty little man. He likes your red hair and amber-green eyes. I'm sure you've noticed that short men like tall women. When they stand in front of you, their eyes zoom in on your bosoms. Haven't you noticed Vince doing that?"

Remy blushed. "I never thought about it."

Later Remy and I returned to the government-run handi-craft and gift shop, where I bought an amethyst ring and an Aztec calendar. Remy bought an Aztec calendar also, as well as two hanging gourds.

"I've got to have that." Remy pointed to a carved teak frieze of a bullfighter. It was three feet wide and about seven inches high. "That would look wonderful on my coffee table."

"How will you get it home?"

"I'll cram it in my suitcase somehow." Remy ran her fingers along the lithe figure of the matador with his cape and toro, head bent to gore the sexy matador.

On Christmas Eve, the square near our hotel was crowded with shoppers. Cars were parked in rows down the middle of the street and on sidewalks in front of department stores. We could have walked across the roofs of cars to cross the street.

We discovered that every restaurant in the vicinity of our hotel was booked. We didn't have a reservation. We thought we might have to forego dinner that evening. Then around 11 p.m., we decided to try the Hotel Alameda's Restaurant 17, which our guidebook recommended.

As we stepped out of the elevator on the 17th floor, the smiling maitre d' greeted us. "*Buenos noches, senoras.*"

Remy touched his arm. "We're starving, but we don't have reservations. Could you possibly accommodate us?"

The man graciously said, "*Si*, of course. I'll see what I can do. Wait just a few moments, *por favor.*"

We gazed out the wall of windows while he set up a small table in the corner of the restaurant. Below was Alameda Central, a landscaped park where people were strolling along well-lit paths. Families sat on benches, children played, lovers held hands, musicians entertained, Indian women sold snacks, and hucksters offered trinkets and balloons.

"This way, *senoras.*" The maitre d' led us to our nook. The menu offered a choice of three Christmas Eve Special Dinners, complete from soup to dessert. We ordered beef tornedos and drinks.

We didn't mind being stuck in the corner; we were lucky to get a table at all. We settled back to watch the large, well-to-do Mexican families, dressed in their fineries, gathered for dinner after Christmas Eve Mass.

While we relished the tender tornedos, the cathedral bells struck midnight and the city was ablaze with fireworks. The meal was expensive—$70 total—but we enjoyed being with the locals for a festive Christmas Eve dinner.

After breakfast at the Pam-Pam Café in Hotel Del Prado on Christmas Day, Jose, our new guide-driver, picked up Remy and me at our hotel for a six-hour tour of the San Juan Teotihuacan pyramids. Four other tourists were already seated in the minivan.

Our first stop was at the Basilica of Guadalupe, Mexico's patron saint.

"We should have invited Angela on this trip. She'd be in her element here," said Remy as we parked in the underground lot of the Buena Vista Railroad Station.

As we crossed the street to the cathedral, Juan said this was the second most visited Catholic shrine. Thousands of people make annual pilgrimages to the church to renew their faith and leave offerings to the Virgin.

As Jose began telling us the tale of Juan Diego, Remy stepped close to him and hung on to his every word.

Jose said that Diego was a peasant who on December 8, 1531,

saw the vision of a brown-skinned, Aztec-speaking Virgin Mary. She was clad in a blue cactus fiber mantle. Later, when he glimpsed the vision again, her image became emblazoned on his cloak. When the bishop saw the image on Juan's cloak, he ordered a church to be built on the spot where Juan had seen the vision.

Remy whispered to me, "I must remember to tell Angela this story."

We entered one of the massive side doors of the basilica and joined other visitors on a moving walkway. We passed behind the altar and saw Juan's cloak hung high on the wall. The cloak was encased in glass, resplendently framed in gold. Within minutes, we were carried to the other side of the altar and out another door.

Outside, local women didn't miss a chance to sell their home-made corn cakes. In the adjacent gift shop, Remy bought a minia-ture statue of the Virgin of Guadalupe for her daughter. "This will be perfect for the small shrine in Jacque's living room. In fact, I should buy one for Angela, too. She has an altar in her house, too."

Back in the minivan, Jose drove along a scenic route to the town of San Juan Teotihuacan. From a distance we could see the pyramids that dominated the horizon. We parked in a large, dusty lot filled with cars, limousines, and tour buses.

After we left the museum/visitors' information building, we walked across a large quadrangle and climbed steps leading to the courtyard of the Temple of Quetzalcoatl, the Toltec god. The struc-ture was decorated with carvings of serpents' heads and goggle-eyed gods.

Sitting on a step of the temple, an Indian woman played tunes on a clay flute. Remy bought one of the flutes, molded in the image of Quetzalcoatl, for her son-in-law. I couldn't resist buying one either. To this day, I haven't been able to produce the clear sweet tones that the woman made look so easy.

Leaving the temple, we drove half a mile to another crowded parking lot close to the Pyramid of the Sun. As we walked toward the pyramid on a dusty dirt path, we passed through a tunnel of vendors selling trashy trinkets. When a man brushed against my breast, I gave him a dirty look. Then one of the beggars gave Remy a pinch on the rear. She turned to him and smiled.

At the base of the Pyramid of the Sun, Jose related a brief history of Teotihuacan, which dated back to 300 B.C. The Toltecs used to sacrifice humans atop the pyramid to gain favor with the gods of wind, earth, fire, and fertility.

When Jose left us on our own, I glanced at the top of the pyramid. I had read in the guidebook that there were 248 steps to the top. Hundreds of people, from babies to the elderly, and their pets, were crawling up the steps like ants for their customary Christmas climb. Parents carried babies in their arms, great-grand-parents leaned on younger persons' arms to make the slow trek upwards. Pet owners carried puppies in their arms, and older dogs bounded easily up the steps ahead of their owners.

Remy and I began our climb. The steps were steep and narrow and badly eroded. At the first terrace, our hearts were pounding. Remy gave up and sat down to wait for me. I charged ahead.

Before I reached the second terrace, I was gasping for breath, my legs were wobbling, and my heart felt like a Mexican jumping bean. Mexico City is more than a mile in altitude, and the pyra-mids are higher. After living in New Orleans, where the highest spot in the city is an overpass on Interstate 10, I wasn't prepared for this altitude. Afraid that I'd have to call the pyramid patrol (similar to a ski patrol, I imagined), I climbed down to join Remy.

We sat on the narrow stone steps and gazed for miles at the ancient ruins and the tranquil valley below. Around us, families were picnicking on grassy spots, a few couples were holding hands, and others were reading newspapers.

"May the curse of the Toltecs haunt our travel agent," I said, fanning the top of my fleece pants suit away from my sweaty chest.

The travel agent had advised us to dress warmly in Mexico because it was December and the city was 7,350 feet high. Obvi-ously, she had never been there in winter. Following the agent's advice, Remy and I had bought fleece pants suits for the trip.

Remy had two sets, one navy blue with a teal collar and stripes across the shoulder and another like it in rose.

"In the next store we come to, I'm going to buy a thin Mexican blouse to wear instead of this fleece thing," I said.

Soon the dust was tickling our noses, so we slowly climbed down to the base of the pyramid. Jose met us and the others in the van and took us into a jewelry shop owned by his friend. I bought an aquamarine ring and Remy bought a gold ring, both modestly priced. Other shops nearby sold sombreros, serapes, sandals, beads, baskets, pottery, mini-pyramids, and postcards.

By then it was three o'clock and we drove to a cantina in Teotihuacan. The large restaurant was decorated with Christmas piñatas, and a mariachi band played syncopated carols. On the front of the marimbas, the musicians had taped a sign reminding us that "Tipping is not a city in China." Along with other busloads of tourists, we enjoyed a spicy buffet and washed it down with Mexican wine or beer.

Back at the hotel, Remy and I showered away the dust of the day, then had drinks in her room before going out for the evening. Remy called room service to ask for ice. Soon a waiter arrived carrying a dish of ice cubes. She tipped him and put the dish on the dresser.

"You're not supposed to drink the water here. Guess that goes for ice cubes too, eh?" Remy said.

I laughed. "We've been drinking the water and using ice cubes for three days. So far, nothing. Guess we're immune or vodka kills the bugs."

"Hope so." We raised our glasses in a toast.

"What's that?" I pointed to a stream of water dripping down the front of the dresser. The water was coming from the ice cubes melting in the metal pan, which was actually a lid with a hole in the center used to keep a plateful of food warm.

"The lousy hotel doesn't even have ice buckets," said Remy. We giggled about that for days.

"Did you ever notice that our Mexican guide looks a little like Vince?"

"No." I frowned. "Well, sort of."

"You know, they're both short, dark men."

"And they like tall redheads, eh?"

Remy blushed.

Later that evening we headed out on foot to the Zona Rosa, an upscale shopping, restaurant, and hotel district two miles away. On the way, we stopped for drinks at the Quorum Lounge in the luxurious Fiesta Palace hotel.

When we reached the Pink Zone, we window-shopped until 10 p.m. We "oohed" and "aahed" at the exquisite and expensive jewels and fashions in the windows. "Dan had the best taste in jewelry. He treated me like a queen." Remy sighed.

We took a taxi back to the Hotel Alameda and ate *cena*, or dinner, at the ground-floor La Brasserie restaurant.

On Friday morning, the 26th, after breakfast at La Brasserie, a third guide-driver, Juan, arrived at our hotel to pick us up in a limousine. Inside, we joined a Dutch banker, his wife, and daughter who were also booked on the all-day tour to Cuernavaca and Taxco, the silver city.

Juan expertly maneuvered the long car up the winding road in the Sierra Madre Mountains to Taxco. There, we ate lunch in a small restaurant that commanded a sweeping view of mountains and silver mines. After shopping for silver and lapis lazuli jewelry and candelabra in Taxco, we visited an old church noted for its historic paintings in Cuernavaca.

Returning to our hotel about 8 p.m., Remy and I again walked to the deluxe Quorum Lounge for cocktails. Then we had a shrimp dinner at the Del Prado Grill.

On our last morning in Mexico City, we decided to get a Mexican breakfast at the crowded La Brasserie. Remy ordered Huevos Rancheros, but I wanted to try menudo, a popular Mexican breakfast dish.

After a few spoonfuls, I frowned. "So much for going native. *No me gusta.*" I motioned for the waiter to take away the dish of tripe soup. "That even smelled awful. You were smart to order that."

Remy said, "I first tasted Huevos Rancheros when Jacquie cooked it for me at her house. It's been my favorite Mexican dish ever since."

Then we walked to Galleria Reforma to spend our last pesos before eating a quick lunch of wine and a Mexican omelet at the Hotel San Francisco. We took a taxi to the airport.

Back in New Orleans at 5:30 p.m., Angela's cousin met us and drove us home. After dinner at the Peking Restaurant, Remy and I drove to Angela's house to say hello, then went to Bruno's to pick up Pooh.

On New Year's Day, Angela and Vince invited Remy and me to join them and two of their children and families to celebrate Bonne Annee. Cajuns believe that by eating cabbage and black-eyed peas on New Year's Day, they are assured of good luck and plenty of greenbacks throughout the new year.

On Dan's birthday, Remy and I spent a quiet evening in my apartment after we had eaten dinner at the Peking Restaurant. Dan would have been sixty-one years old.

In February, a week before Fat Tuesday, the police went on strike. The mayor and his council met to decide what to do about Mardi Gras. They did not want to risk the safety of citizens, visitors, and Mardi Gras krewes by allowing the parade to go on without police protection. Past history had demonstrated that policemen on horseback patrolling the parade route and the French Quarter were major deterrents to crime. Consequently, the Mardi Gras parades were canceled for the first time since World War II.

Work at the Navy Facility went on as usual. I found my job easy, and I enjoyed putting out the monthly newspaper. It didn't take me long to gather canned news, a few syndicated features and photos, and lay out the paper each month. A Navy public affairs office was a far cry from the long-ago newsrooms, where glazed doughnuts and black coffee reigned supreme and fifths of bourbon were stashed in bottom desk drawers.

The Navy Facility had all the ingredients for a soap opera stew. Mix a couple of cups of attractive widows and single women with a cup or two of rising Naval aviators, already bored with their tired wives and screaming toddlers, or horny singles, and a quarter of a cup of work in common to talk about, three-martini lunches or happy hours at the clubs, and stir. Somebody was bound to fall in love, have a hot affair, or a one-night stand.

Lola, the public affairs secretary, who swore me to secrecy, told me that our captain liked her to stay after hours and take dictation——while sitting on his lap. He made sure those sessions were long enough to satisfy his need.

Each month Jacob and I had to take the newspaper's camera-ready layout sheets to the job shop on Tchoupitoulas Street, in the central business district of New Orleans.

While waiting for the paper to be printed, we'd usually eat lunch at Mother's Restaurant. Every noon, hungry diners eagerly lined up at Mother's, which featured po'boys, biscuits and gravy, grits, ham, turkey, jambalaya, etouffee, red beans and rice, and seafood. Customers ate standing at counters or, if they arrived early, they could sit at the few tables in the restaurant.

One day while Jacob and I were eating there, he asked, "Do you fool around?"

"What do you mean?"

"You know, sex. With men like me." His smile was as insincere as the grin on a garish Mardi Gras mask.

"Ha! You're married."

"Oh, it's all in fun."

"No way, Jose. Not with married men and definitely not with my boss. I even obey speed limits and Keep Off the Grass signs." I didn't want to be the subject of office gossip around the water cooler or over martini lunches.

Jacob never brought up the subject again.

On Saturdays, Remy and I usually went shopping at D.J. Holmes and other department stores in downtown New Orleans. We lingered over lunches, as was the way in the Vieux Carre.

Some days Remy and I would buy Muffalettas at a grocery

store on Decatur Street. Those Italian sandwiches, similar to po'boys and hoagies, seemed to be designed to eat while sitting on the benches of the Moon Walk beside the Mississippi River.

While eating, we'd watch the pigeons hopping on the levee.

"Look at that Romeo." I pointed to a male pigeon, his chest feathers all plumped up into iridescent purples and pinks, vainly trying to woo a lady pigeon who kept walking away from him and pecking at the pavement.

"She couldn't care less," said Remy.

"I kind of feel sorry for him," I said. "He looks so sad as he gives up. Reminds me of a man whose fiancé just broke their engagement."

On one Saturday morning we went to Remy's favorite jewelers. He welcomed Remy and expressed sorrow at her loss. Dan had purchased all his gifts for Remy in this shop. Remy asked the jeweler if he could design a gold-chained pendant using the large diamonds from her engagement and wedding rings. He said he could do that and have it ready in about two weeks.

Another morning, Remy drove me to the West End park on Lake Ponchartrain. We walked on the boardwalk and stopped for fried oysters at a restaurant built out over the lake. The lake shone metallic cobalt-blue, as flat as a coin and stretched north as far as we could see. Several boats skimmed the surface in the middle of the lake.

"In summer, there's an amusement park here with a ferris wheel and a tunnel of love," Remy said. "Everybody walks around carrying plastic statuettes of Mae West or stuffed alligators they won at shooting galleries or carnival games."

"I heard Pete Fountain has a country home across the lake, is that true?" My eyes followed the causeway that stretches 24 miles across the lake.

"Yes. The northshore is a different country. Fresh air, pine woods, wetlands, and estates of wealthy New Orleaneans. There're also art galleries, antique shops, and bed and breakfast inns."

"Sounds wonderful. I'll bet houses there are expensive."

Remy laughed. "You could say that, but if you have to ask, you can't afford one. Rex Rampart, his wife, and three children live in a plantation house there, too."

"Have you ever been there?"

"Yes. Dan and I were invited to Rex's party to celebrate Vince and Angela's thirtieth wedding anniversary. His house is surrounded by lawns, oaks, swimming pool, tennis court, gazebo, two guest cottages, and a garden fountain. He said that the bricks in the house were dug from clay pits and baked in kilns by slaves in the 1790s."

"Wow. It sounds luxurious."

"Some day we'll take a drive around the lake. I'll show you Rex's place."

Lent was over and New Orleans was dazzling with April's soft light and color. Magnolia blossoms covered trees like colored powder puffs. Azaleas took over when tulips left off.

One day at lunch in the Chief's Club, Remy confided in me that she often woke up in the morning and stretched out her hand to the other side of the bed. Nothing. Her fingers trembled. Dan was gone somewhere forever where she couldn't follow, leaving behind a tender hole in her heart.

On the first anniversary of Dan's death in April, Remy, Angela, Ellen, and I drove to Biloxi to visit Dan's grave.

Remy drove west on U.S. Highway 90, called The Strip, the asphalt road along the Gulf of Mexico. The road lies atop ancient ruts of the Old Spanish Trail, the route of smugglers and thieves for three centuries. The lush spring air that blew in from the Gulf embraced us with a cleansing tang, a taste of gritty brine mixed with magnolias and sea oats. The murky, lukewarm water here along the coast was the color of cognac.

"I always liked Biloxi," said Angela. "My parents used to bring me here on weekends. We didn't mind the decay, things falling apart, the crap along the beaches, the skeletons of abandoned hotels, the trashy warehouses, and rundown piers jutting out into the dirty water."

I laughed. "You make it sound terrible."

"Still, it's charming."

"This is where the honkies tonked," Remy added.

"Oooh."

On the north side of the highway sat symbols of the genteel South, of small-town boosterism for the military, of wealth and grace and the glorious past, all mingled with the Strip's squalid hodgepodge of striptease joints and miniature golf, cheap motels, fast-food restaurants, and bars.

We traveled past Beauvoir, the estate owned by Confederate president Jefferson Davis. Now it's a retirement-home-tour-bus-stop. We continued past the mothballed Air Force jet skewered atop a giant pylon and plopped onto the median like a child's model, and past beachfront antebellum mansions with white columns and oak trees bearded with Spanish moss.

Biloxi's waterfront, with its shrimp boats, ramshackle buildings, aging docks, offshore oil rigs permeated with the aroma of rotting fish floating atop oily black waters, was being redeveloped. Most of the old shrimp-canning factories were closed, but in some, old women still snapped the heads off shrimp before canning them.

Biloxi, founded in 1699, was the home of the Dixie Mafia, no relation to the Sicilian Mafia, and a drug-running sheriff. The coastal strip of the '60s and '70s was a hotbed of burglary, theft, illegal gambling, liquor violations, swindling, forgery, and grand larceny.

A narrow beach of bright white sand separated the four lanes of blacktop from the steel blue arc of the Gulf. The beach was artificial, its sand dredged up from the sea bottom and sprayed on the rocky shore like stucco. Residents of the area have been paying a tax for this transplanted sand for the past 30 years. Alligators and snakes lived in murky waters of the back bay, along the gutters of roads and in golf course traps.

By the time we arrived in Biloxi, it was noon, and we were hungry. We ate lunch at Mary Mahoney's Old French House Restaurant and Old Slave Quarters Lounge, a historic building housing the restaurant and gift shop on Magnolia and Water Streets.

"Never on Sundays," is the owner's slogan. The restaurant is among Biloxi's twenty historic buildings, which include Greek Revival to French Colonial styles of the 1700s and 1800s.

Over martinis, Remy recalled how she and Dan always ate lunch there when they came to shop at the commissary or to visit doctors or dentists at Keesler Air Force Base.

"I read somewhere that Elvis Presley used to come here to fish in the mid-1950s," I said.

"Yes," Ellen said. "And Oscar Wilde often visited Jefferson Davis at his home a century before that. Jayne Mansfield also made pilgrimages to Biloxi. Did you know that she was decapitated in an automobile accident on Highway 90. Her 'death car' used to be displayed here, but then it was moved to Las Vegas."

"Mary Mahoney's is famous for her bread pudding," said Remy.

"I can see why," I said as I tasted the rum-soaked bread pudding. "This is to die for. I'd like to get the recipe."

"You can pick up the recipe at the counter. Mary loves to share it with customers," said Ellen.

After lunch, we drove to the National Cemetery.

I helped Remy carry a small cooler from the trunk of the car to Dan's grave.

Fortunately, the day was sunny and the ground was dry, in contrast to the soggy spectacle the year before when Dan was buried. Remy bent down and pulled some weeds that had grown up around the grave. She put the weeds, along with some old flowers, in a nearby trash can.

Remy reached into the cooler and pulled out four glasses and a vacuum bottle full of martinis. She filled the glasses and handed them to us.

"To Dan." We raised our glasses in unison.

Remy whispered, "Without you, Dan, there's no me. Have a drink, sweetheart." She poured her martini over Dan's grave.

"Guess he's enjoying that big Mardi Gras in the sky," said Angela.

"Oooh." Ellen patted Remy's arm.

"That's where I'll be laid to rest. I'll be with Dan again." Remy pointed to the empty spot beside Dan's grave. She threw him a kiss.

CHAPTER SIX

Spring was hot in New Orleans even though May was only a few days old. The calendar claimed summer was still six weeks away, but the delta knew better. Blossoms had burst, new leaves were vibrant green, and the air was heavily perfumed. The sky outlined around the buildings was tender blue, almost turquoise, clothing the city in an ethereal atmosphere.

On spring days in the French Quarter, battle lines are drawn between artists who've displayed their works around Jackson Square for generations and a new wave of musicians, performers, and psychics whose antics shatter the repose of nearby residents and draw tourist dollars from the artists' pockets.

One Friday evening, Remy asked whether I wanted to go with her to a singles' dance held at the Desire Ballroom in Metairie. Of course, I wanted to go. I hadn't danced in years and I liked the prospect of meeting some interesting men. I had read announcements of the singles dances in the newspaper, but I wouldn't dream of going alone.

I walked to Remy's apartment and knocked on the door.

"It's open," Remy called.

In the foyer, I asked, "Where are you?"

"In the bedroom, Grace. Would you make me a dressin' drink, please? Make yourself one too."

"A dressin' drink?"

"Yeah. A drink while I finish dressing. It's a Southern thing."

I made two vodkas and water and took them into the bedroom. I sat in the chaise lounge while Remy, sitting at her vanity table, put the finishing touches on her makeup. The music box on the vanity tinkled, "When you wish upon a star, your dreams come true."

The vitality of spring rushed through Remy's veins. She seemed to be getting over Dan's death, at least on the surface.

Remy had taken good care of herself. At 56, there wasn't a wrinkle on her face, and she needed only a dab of powder and rouge. She was chic, with the height of a showgirl, and a graceful way of moving her head, sweeping a wisp of her short bob off her face with long fingers and painted nails.

"Do you think you'll ever fall in love again?" I asked Remy.

She turned to look at me. "I suppose so. People do. But my heart says no."

"It's too bad that true, long-lasting love is so hard to find in this hectic world. People seem to change partners like they're playing musical chairs these days. Of course, who am I to talk, with three marriages under my belt. Not to change the subject, but I love that Mickey Mouse phone on the bedside table."

"So do I," Remy smiled. "Dan and I got it at Disney World years ago. Guess it's the child in me."

"Maybe in all of us."

"That should do." Remy dabbed Opium perfume on her neck, wrists, and between her breasts. "Opium used to drive Dan wild." She stood up and turned around. She was wearing a dark purple full skirt and a sheer pink blouse with a deep Vee neck.

"You're not going out like that, are you?"

Remy blushed. Her nipples projected like lighthouse beams through her sheer pink blouse. "This is the latest style bra from Victoria's Secret. The nipples are cut out."

"Yeah, I can see that. No wonder you get more dances than I do. You look too good for a woman whose husband is so recently gone."

Remy grimaced. "Did you think my hair would turn white

and wrinkles would spring out on my face? Dan died, darlin', I didn't."

I didn't answer her, but I was glad she was taking that attitude.

Remy liked designer clothes: Jordache stretch jeans, Beverly Hills Polo club T-shirts, Dior sunglasses, and Gucci bags. When Remy walked over to close the closet doors, I saw that the floor was covered with shoes of all colors and descriptions.

"Are you sure you have enough shoes?"

Remy laughed. "Years of wearing designer shoes with pointed toes and stiletto heels made my feet crooked. Now I can only wear shoes with round toes or open sandals. When I find shoes that fit me, I buy several pairs in various colors. Like those demi-boots I wear to work."

"I've wanted to ask you about those boots. I like them. Where do you get them?"

"I order them from Old Pueblo Traders catalog. I must have every color they sell. I'll give you one of my catalogs."

"Thanks."

"I love shoes, but I don't think I have as many pairs of shoes as Imelda Marcos."

On the drive to the ballroom, I sighed. "I'm nervous. I've always loved to dance, but this is my first singles thing in years. Hope someone asks me to dance."

"Don't worry, they will. Of course, there are never enough men to go around. I'll warn you though, look out for married men who are single for the night, hoping to get lucky."

"My mother used to say that dancing shows you what a man is going to do before he does it."

As we pulled into the oyster-shell parking lot of the Desire Ballroom, the rain started. Though the block-square lot was almost full, Remy found a place close to the entrance. The ballroom was in a renovated warehouse in Metairie, in a respectable middle-class area away from the city center.

Music drew us like a magnet the minute we stepped out of the car. The ballroom opened at eight o'clock, and a line of men and women had formed outside. In the light sprinkle, Remy and I stood behind the others waiting to pay the $3 admission fee.

Within minutes we stepped inside, where one of the two bands had struck up "Tuxedo Junction." The dance hall featured two eight-piece bands, each on a stage at opposite ends of the ballroom. One band wore red tuxedos and the other blue. The bands alternated playing sets.

The lights were low in the room, but two large glass balls spun slowly from the ceiling, emitting waves of scarlet, blue, and green ripples across the heads of the dancers. The music stopped, the lights were turned up, and the floor started to clear in the hiatus when one band finished a set and the other began to play.

Remy and I went to the bar and ordered vodkas on the rocks with twists. We leaned against the bar and surveyed the crowd.

"This is like a supermarket. Just look at the humanity on the dance floor. Fat, thin, blond, brunette, from downright ugly to ravishing," I said. "You name it, they're here. Men must have a field day here, with so many women fighting over them. Guess if a man has a pulse, a driver's license and can dance, women will be all over him like vultures."

"Yeah. That's why it's called a meat market, m-e-a-t."

"You mean, everybody looks over every body else like they're appraising carcasses hanging in an abattoir."

Remy pointed to an empty table on the edge of the dance floor, and we hurried to claim it before someone else did.

Following a few steps behind Remy, I noticed that her coppery hair was set afire by the glimmery light from the glass balls on the ceiling. Every man in the room noticed her, of course, as she strode towards the table like the queen of the ballroom, with a model's graceful glide, pelvis tilted, head erect. She walked with avidity, as though she were lurching headlong toward a gala picnic of sex. Remy knew she was being noticed. She reached up and straightened the diamond heart hanging from her gold necklace.

We had been seated only a few minutes when a man asked

Remy to dance. He took her in his arms at the table and danced her to the center of the floor. They were holding each other close, her nose against his chin, her left hand around his neck. His hand was on Remy's back, his fingers spread across her waist.

During the intermission, Remy brought her dance partner to our table. Their heads were together and they were speaking in a low, intimate way, like lovers who, having been long parted, had much to tell each other. Remy's voice was as intimate as the rustle of silk sheets. She modulated her voice so it was never loud, never strident, a bit soft so that a man has to lean close to listen.

Not only was Remy a strikingly pretty woman, she had early on perfected wiles useful in reducing men to putty. Since many men were not as tall as Remy, she mastered the disarming habit of lowering her eyes, then raising them as though only the object of her glance could promise a welcome, intimate response. While chatting with a man, she teased him by running her fingertips over his hand. Lowering her shoulder a tad in his direction also sparked fire in a male. She was seducing him. That these were calculated postures, as studied as an actress's blocking on the stage, never occurred to men.

Remy had men lined up to dance with her. I got the leftovers. I used to tell Remy, "You sure give me the creeps."

Then I was asked to dance. I put one hand on the man's shoulder and felt his arm slide behind my neck, his body pressing against mine on the turns. He smelled of whiskey. When the band played a tango, the floor suddenly cleared. I thanked the man and returned to the table. I didn't want to dance again with him, especially not a romantic tango.

I danced with another man but it was living hell. I gagged on his body odor. I waited until the number ended and mumbled, "I'm going to the little girls room." On the other side of the dance floor, I breathed clean air, even though a blue haze filtered from the smokers at the bar.

The Blue Band's leader announced that the next number was a Ladies' Choice, which took place every hour. Most men waited, chatting with friends, seemingly unconcerned. Remy dashed to one of her ballroom Romeos.

Now here's my chance, I thought. I lost no time approaching a nice-looking man I had spotted earlier. I knew he was a smooth dancer. I enjoyed my first good dance of the evening.

When the band switched moods to "Ballin' the Jack," the floor became as rowdy as a fairground. Couples jiggled and writhed to the throbbing bass music.

Then the band played "September Song." The glass balls in the ceiling cast rippling waves across the dancing couples. I watched the matches taking shape, exchanging names, the awkward flirting, meeting strangers, dancing intimately, momentarily abandoning inhibitions in the neutral meeting place of the dance floor. Laughing merrily, they paraded back and forth in front of the mirrored walls of the ballroom.

At eleven o'clock, the two bands played, in unison, "Goodnight Ladies" and then "Auld Lang Syne." This signaled the end of the evening, and people began to leave the ballroom.

Many couples paired up, men offered to drive women home, or hoped to be invited to their homes. Those whose luck ran out went home alone. Remy seldom went home alone, unless she chose to. Sometimes she and her escort stopped by a bar in East New Orleans; other times she'd invite them to her apartment for cuddling, touchy-feely and, as far as I knew, nothing more.

During the next few months, Remy and I attended the dances at the Desire Ballroom each weekend. The evenings were fun, a good excuse to dress up, and get a little exercise. Neither of us met anyone we wanted to see outside of the dances. Most single men our ages, if they weren't gay, had bad breath and body odor, were too poor to date, or had one foot in the grave.

One day Remy and Ellen invited me to join them for lunch at the Chief's Club.

The women were bosom buddies, though they were as different as apples and oysters. Remy was originally from New York City and Ellen was a native New Orleanian. Their common links, of course, were working for the Navy Facility and their love of dry martinis and five-star restaurants. The third member of their circle was Angela Santorini. The women went everywhere together during and after working hours, always in Remy's car because neither Ellen nor Angela drove. The three friends had lost count of the years among them; they'd known each other for almost two decades. In time, the material differences among them had eroded, but their individual characters and mutual interests remained. After a few martinis, they called themselves the *femmi de parti* for their love of the good life.

Ellen, Angela, and I were determined to keep Remy busy, to fill her after-work hours with interesting activities to keep her mind off Dan.

One Saturday the gang of four, as my boss Jacob called us, booked an all-day bayou tour.

A strong breeze had kicked up behind thick layers of morning clouds. Spring had been like summer, the days and nights were so hot and humid there was mildew on our shoes each morning. By noon the sun made the goldenrod glisten and drove the gnats and flies into a frenzy to find cool shade.

We took seats along the rail under a canopy, in the shade. Recorded Cajun-French songs, featuring a guitar and an accordion, were piped over the loud speaker as the shallow-hulled paddlewheel boat glided slowly through the swamp and bayous, minutes from downtown, but centuries away.

The boat cut the water with hardly a sound as we slipped along the shore through sluggish waters and into a dusty tunnel of towering boughs of cypress. The topmost branches were thin and covered with silvery webs woven by spiders or silkworms. Spanish moss that trailed over low hanging branches resembled the antebellum lace-draped arms of curtsying belles.

Over the speaker, the guide related the history of the Cajuns. This was pirate country, he said, the stomping ground for Jean LaFitte, one of the deadliest pirates in the West Indies and the Gulf of Mexico. LaFitte had a shop on Royal Street in the Quarter and a sumptuous house furnished with loot from ships he had waylaid.

"Oooh. Look." Ellen pointed to a grotesquely shaped cypress tree ten feet thick and thirty feet tall, its thick trunk forming a fluted wedge rising from the water. The cypresses had grown so close together that the sun could find its way through only in patches, backlighting the gray shrouds of moss flourishing in the branches. Scattered between the trees were walls of cypress knees four feet high. Knees were used to make lamps and clocks to sell to tourists.

"Ah, *eau de bayou*," I said, inhaling the sweet aromas of magnolias, trumpet flowers, and wild honeysuckle that mingled with earthier odors of rotting vegetation and Gulf salt drifting on the humid air. A greenish gloom pervaded everything that lay around the boat.

"It's too quiet here," said Angela. "It's eerie."

The silence around us gave me a sense of distance from any world I knew. Soon the quiet was broken by owls greeting the sun with demoniac laughter, cranes whooping, woodpeckers drumming, and bright red birds croaking their hoarse swampsongs in the veiled mist of gnats and mosquitos as the murky water moved against the side of the paddlewheeler.

The coastal plain was a wildlife sanctuary where hundreds of migratory birds came to roost. Ospreys, egrets, pelicans, ducks, cranes, and geese took cover in the marshy refuge. A dozen white herons and a Louisiana brown pelican, perched on the brink of extinction, flew low across the bow of the boat.

"I feel like I'm swimming in a tropical fish tank," I said.

As we floated along, we were being observed by alligators, nutria, and birds. The water was alive with crawfish, shrimp, oysters, red snappers, flounder, pompano, bream, crags, and alligators. Frogs croaked, gators roared and slithered over the cool mud, nutria and muskrats scurried frantically around.

"What are nutria?" I asked.

"They're furry rodents. In the 1930s, swamp ranchers brought the nutria here in hopes of selling the pelts as middle-class mink," Angela said.

"If I remember correctly, the McIlhenneys of Tabasco sauce fame, imported a dozen nutria from Argentina," Ellen added. "Now there's about three million nutria in the bayous."

"Does anyone eat nutria?" I asked.

"Nutria gumbo? Guess it'd be okay smothered in Tabasco sauce," Angela cackled.

"Oooh."

Dozens of snakes were entwined together in clumps or were slicing through the water like green and brown threads. Snakes, gray, thick-bodied, vile, were coiled around nearly every cypress knee and lower tree branches.

"We're entering Alligator Alley," the boat guide announced. "Maybe we'll get lucky and see El Whoppo."

"What's that?"

Angela cackled. "The biggest gator in the swamp."

"Oooh."

"There it is." The guide's voice cracked with electricity and he pointed to El Whoppo cruising towards the starboard side of the boat. "It's a gator of biblical proportions, fourteen feet long weighing a thousand pounds."

"Big enough to swallow up people," Remy said.

We sat transfixed and speechless as Whoppo's full body surfaced and he opened his gargantuan jaws. Then the giant gator slogged into the thick cover of the bayou.

A four-foot-long alligator with a crimpled white heron in its jaws sat on the decaying length of a fallen tree. A longer gator drifted past, its cat-green eyes and ridged skull visible as its snout pushed through the foul brown water. Occasionally, two or three gators would bump together in their back-and-forth loglike driftings and there was an instant's outburst of thrashing anger, but then everything would calm down again.

"I wouldn't want to be stranded here, not even in a boat," I said.

"Look out there," said Remy. "That floating log is the bulk and snout of a gator. I sure don't want to go swimming here."

"Did you know that gators can't bite under water?" Angela tried to allay our fears. "They seldom attack humans except in self-defense, and they don't go after things larger than themselves. They can't see well to the sides, either."

As to their reputed harmlessness, every lowcountry native had a story about the cat, the dog, the small child snatched from the bank by those scalloped jaws. Around the bayous, the nubs of a hand or foot are said to have been taken by alligators. The shelf life of poodles and shih tzus wasn't long in the lagoon homesites. Gators look ponderous, dragging their scaled hugeness on short, bent legs, but they can move like lightning, can be down a bank and into the water in the flicker of an eye.

"I read in the paper that smugglers stuff dead alligators with drugs and ship them north to their contacts," I said.

"Oooh."

The guide droned on, a little monotonously, about the history of the bayous.

For centuries a quiet battle of nature had raged without interference along the coastline of what would become Louisiana. From the south, the ocean pushed inland with its tides and winds and floods. From the north, the Mississippi hauled down an inexhaustible supply of freshwater and sediment, and fed the marshes with the soil they needed to vegetate and thrive. The river slowly built a long succession of deltas, each of which in turn blocked the river's path and forced it to change course, leaving vast wetlands.

Before the discovery of oil in the Mississippi Delta, the forces of nature were in control. Some of the richest soil on Earth was deposited over eons of Aprils when the Mississippi River overflowed its banks. Each time the river withdrew, it left behind more topsoil.

When oil was discovered there in 1930, companies dredged 10,000 miles of canals to get to the riches. They crisscrossed the fragile delta with a slashing array of neat little ditches. They drilled, found oil, then dredged like maniacs to get to it. Their canals were perfect conduits for the Gulf and its saltwater, which ate away at the marshes.

"Speaking of oil reminds me of Huey Long. I once met the Kingfish, as he called himself," said Ellen.

"I've heard of Long, but I don't know much about him." I was sure Ellen could fill me in. It always amazed me how Ellen could come up with so many little tidbits of history. She missed her calling; she should have been a historian instead of a secretary.

"He ran the Louisiana parishes like a set of toy trains. After serving as governor, and near dictator, Kingfish arrived in Washington as a U.S. Senator around 1921, I believe. Long hated Standard Oil and opposed the big oil moguls who ruined these wetlands. He dreamed of wearing his orange ties and smoking cigars in the White House, but he never made it."

"What happened to him?" I asked.

"He was murdered by a doctor who thought Long was a tyrant and believed his father-in-law had been wronged by Long's political organization. The doctor who shot Long with a Belgian .32 was then killed by Long's bodyguards. Long's grave sits in the garden behind the state capitol in Baton Rouge, where Long was assassinated."

"It's so peaceful floating in the bayou," said Remy. "There's no hurry to get anywhere."

Big metal piroques, their long sticks anchored to the side, dipped, pushed, and glided past the riverboat. A lift of the pole and the flat-bottom boat slipped forward fast. They're so light, narrow, and draw such little water that Cajuns say they float on the dew.

"Yes. Bayou country reminds me of truth," said Ellen. "The strongest trees, like truth, are ones whose roots go the deepest. If the roots aren't deep enough, or false, they get washed away in floods and by the wind."

"I can picture Mark Twain, traveling down dark waters with his sun-burned cronies, reveling in freebooting lives of pirates filled with rum, reaching for wenches, grabbing asses, laughing," I said.

At one o'clock we bought soft-shell crab po'boys, served in plastic lattice baskets, and bottles of Dixie beer from the snack bar on the lower deck.

Before the boat docked, Remy and I visited the gift shop on the main deck. We each bought a metal music box in the shape of a paddlewheeler and a poster that lamented, "Do You Know What It Means To Miss New Orleans?"

Remy and I would find out soon enough how it felt to be away from the Big Easy.

CHAPTER SEVEN

One Friday afternoon at work, I asked Remy whether she was going dancing that evening.

"No. I met someone special last night. I stopped by the Do Drop Inn after dinner and met a tall Cajun. Can he dance! Not like a professional, but lively. He walked up to me and said, I've been watching you. I've gotta say, WOW! What a pickup line, eh?"

"It must have worked. Tell me about him."

"His name is Beauregard Xavier Bovier, but everyone calls him Beau. He's a gentleman, in a Cajun way. He's the maintenance supervisor at a Catholic girls' school in the Garden District. He has to drive fifty miles every day from his house in the Rigolets. He has a teenage son called 'Tit Gard, a nickname meaning *petit*, or little Beauregard. Anyway, we danced until late, then came back to my apartment. We're going out again tonight."

"I'd like to meet him."

"I'll take you to his house soon. He's always inviting friends and neighbors in for shrimp and oysters. He loves to cook for company."

One Saturday in the middle of June, Remy and I drove to Beau's house, or camp as he called it, near the Rigolets, a series of bayous and swamps where Louisiana and Mississippi meet.

Traditionally, Cajun camps were built on islands or backed up to bayous, Creole style. They began as humble shacks for trappers and oystermen in the marshes, swamps, or woods. Some were nothing more than shrimp-drying platforms. As the need to get far away from civilization for hunting and fishing increased, many families built camps for recreation and sports.

The farther from New Orleans we drove, the more inlets we passed where masts and riggings of battered shrimp boats, with rubber tires as fenders, bobbed on the waves created by passing skiffs. We drove past swampy lots with tin-roofed fishing shacks built on stilts.

On the way, Remy told me about Beau. "His Cajun roots are sunk deep into delta dirt, as he likes to say. He says French was his cradle language. He has a wonderful sense of humor. Says it keeps him cool and loose about things, but he has a zest for life. Beau claims he's no more hot and robust than any other Cajun."

"Ah yes, let the good times roll." I shifted in the seat and watched the small businesses pass by on Chef Menteur highway.

Both sides of the road were lined with stores that hawked Boat Repair—Fiberglass Speciality, Hard Shell Crabs 4 Sale, JAX Best Beer in Town, NEHI, Duke's Choice Chewing Tobacco, Gas. Other signs advertised Cajun goodies—boudin, cracklins, Andouille, tasso, nachos, frito pies, hamburgers, chili dogs, po'boys. Try our fresh, homemade Cajun egg rolls.

Most stores, only about 15 by 20 feet, sported sloping concrete steps, false fronts of warped and paintless clapboard, cracked plateglass windows mended with lightning-bolt adhesive tape. Hand-lettered signs at the top read Groceries. Some stores had sliding glass windows in front so the owners could serve beer, homemade "susage," and hot "boodin" to walk-up customers.

On the porches of mom-and-pop groceries, men wearing canvas hats, dirty T-shirts, and sneakers sat on old car seats. They each had one big hand wrapped around Dixie beer bottles.

"There's his pickup." Remy turned south onto a dead-end dirt road and parked on Beau's driveway, a swath of broken oyster shells. As we walked towards the camp, the shells crunched beneath our feet. We crossed a narrow, sandy yard that surrounded the house.

"*Bonjour*, y'all," Beau called as he came out from under the house. He strode to Remy and gave her a hug that was almost obscene. He was several inches taller than Remy. He had a beer belly as round as the Gulf of Mexico, atop skinny legs. I guessed he was a few years younger than Remy.

When Remy introduced me, Beau gave me a bear hug. "Welcome to my camp."

His house, erected on cypress pillars, had a pitched roof, a style borrowed years ago from the West Indies. Since his divorce three years ago, Beau had been upgrading his fishing camp, turning it into a comfortable home. On the ground beneath the house was an outdoor kitchen and berths for two boats. The main part of the house, reached by steep wooden steps, contained a livingroom, two bedrooms, two baths, a modern kitchen, and a back porch that overlooked the bayou. Remy had bought some curtains, throw rugs, and a few cushions to give the place a woman's touch.

That afternoon, Beau took us for a ride in his motorboat. As he helped us into the boat, he said he caught shrimp, crawfish, and catfish in those waters. "You'll love my fried catfish," he said to me.

The day was windless. Water lay thick as black glass, dotted here and there with silver or bronze where a shaft of sunshine pierced the darkness. In its calm depths, drowsing alligators lurked and dreadful cottonmouths slithered. There was a slight mulchy, fishy smell in the swamp.

"You can eat everything in the bayou, and vice versa," said Beau. "Don't worry about snakes. Even if they drop into the boat, they're more afraid of you than you are of them."

The boat skimmed across the still water, past islands of cypress knees and copses of sweet-smelling water hyacinths and magnolia blossoms the size of dinner plates.

"Have you ever been lost here?" I asked.

"No. I know it by heart. But there's no east, west, north, or south in the bayou, just up and down the bayou."

An hour later, Beau pulled the boat into a berth below his

house. As we stepped inside, I said. "Something smells good."

"Before we went out, I put a pot of shrimp jambalaya on the stove to simmer."

"Good thinking. What a pretty tablecloth." I ran my hand over the blue-and-white Fleur de Lis cloth on Beau's kitchen table.

"A neighbor lady gave me that when I started living here full time."

"Isn't this France's icon?"

"Yes. It's also a symbol for the Trinity. Fleur de Lis is dear to the hearts of us Cajuns."

"That's an unusual knife you're using." I pointed to the blade, embellished with a detailed buffalo on the prairie.

Beau used the knife to pick out the black vein from a shrimp the size of his fist. "It's a Bowie knife, named after brothers Jim and Rezin Bowie. Jim was a colonel in the Texas army. He died at the Alamo. It's a traditional frontier knife, with an especially honed six-inch blade of stainless steel. A hunter wouldn't be caught dead without his Bowie."

Beau held up the knife and winked. "It's also called an Arkansas toothpick."

"That's interesting," I laughed.

"Stick by me, gal, you'll learn a lot." Beau winked again. "Did you know shrimp caught around oil rigs grow to gumbo size? Whatever the rigs are dumping into the Gulf makes the shrimp grow like crazy."

During the next year, I frequently accompanied Remy to Beau's house for a weekend. I enjoyed the raw oysters, fried shrimp, and catfish feasts that Beau staged, and I didn't mind sleeping overnight on the livingroom sofa.

One afternoon I said to Beau, "I hear you make a delicious chocolate bread pudding."

"*Oui*," he winked. "In fact, I made Remy my famous pudding the first night she stayed over."

"What's so special about it, other than it's made with chocolate?"

"Nothing. It's so easy. I just tear up half a loaf of stale French bread into bite-size pieces, beat the hell out of eggs and sugar, add melted chocolate, and mix it all nice and pretty with my hands. Last, with a little hip wiggle, I stir in a cup of brandy. Then bake."

On Sunday mornings, Beau liked to cook his favorite breakfast: Andouille Islands, hen eggs and sausage cooked with cayenne pepper, Cajun spices, and Andouille sausage. He served it with grits, potatoes, or biscuits.

He mixed Bloody Mary drinks with layers of brandy at the bottom, tequila, and lime with raw egg broken on top. "Good for hangovers," Beau claimed.

"I'll say." The drink cleared my head like a plumber's snake clears a drain pipe.

After breakfast, I'd clean up the kitchen while Remy and Beau, and his son if he was there, would attend service at the local Baptist Church. Beau cut a handsome figure in his Sunday morning best suit. I knew Remy wasn't particularly religious, but she went to church to please Beau. She told me once that she and Dan had always planned to return to regular Sunday services, but they never got around to it.

Sometimes on weekends we played records on Beau's old phonograph. The three of us, and some of his neighbors, danced together around the picnic table on the ground below the house.

"Here's a rare piece of Pete Fountain's," said Beau, putting on a record. "It's called 'Sunday in the Country.'"

"I like that one," said Remy. "This is about the only record Pete's made where he sings. He's not a good singer."

I listened to Pete crooning. The song opens with church bells ringing. Then the few words extol Sunday dinner in the country with biscuits and fried chicken. He didn't have a good voice, but he could be forgiven because he sure could tickle the clarinet.

"Here's one of my favorites," said Beau, placing a recording of "Jambalaya" on the record player. "It's one of Hank Williams biggest hits. He based it on the two-step called Grand Texas or L'Anse Couche-couche."

When Beau danced it was pure Louisiana: flat-footed, spraddle-legged, smooth glides, twisting hands scratching the air, boots winking and zapping across boards, long muscled legs bending and digging, swiveling hip sockets. He knew a hundred dance steps echoing the buzzard lope, Texas Tommy, the grind, funky butt, twist, Charleston, and the shimmy.

"You can really dance, Beau," I said.

"It's in my blood. I may have snow on my roof, but there's still a fire in my belly." He winked at Remy.

One evening Remy and Beau were cuddling on the sofa and I was watching a mystery on television. I overheard their conversation.

"You sure were good last night."

Remy blushed. "You weren't bad yourself."

"I can tell it's you even in the dark."

"How?"

"By your smell."

"What?"

"When you get excited, your pussy smells like the bayou, you know, shrimp or ersters."

"Well, we do eat a lot of raw oysters."

"Makes me virile, *oui*? Champagne and ersters—the feast of love. They say they're aphrodisiacs."

Remy laughed. "Where did you learn that word?"

"I'm not just a dumb Cajun. I read a lot."

"I know you do. You're filled with contradictions. That's why I like you."

"Love and food go hand in hand," said Beau.

"What do you mean?" I asked.

"Salmon arouses me. Just think of the struggling salmon swimming their way home upstream against the current to find their mate."

It had taken Remy a year to accept Dan's death. She stopped feeling guilty about going on living. A week after she met Beau, she quietly slipped off her wedding ring.

The Friday afternoon before Labor Day, a traditional change of command ceremony for the Navy Facility was held aboard the *USS Lexington*, an aircraft carrier moored for the occasion at the foot of Canal Street in New Orleans.

The Navy had held a public open house the day before the ceremony, but that afternoon it was closed except to Navy employees, local dignitaries, and guests. Navy civilian employees were given the afternoon off, and if they didn't want to attend, they had to stay at work. My boss had to write up the change of command for our paper, and the Chief was going to take pictures. Of course, all of the public affairs staff went to the ceremony. It's well known that writers never pass up free food and drinks.

Of course, Ellen had a hand in organizing the event. The ceremony was held on the Lexington's flight deck with Navy A-7B aircraft, with the skyline of New Orleans and the Mississippi River as backdrops. The ship was the platform for the change of command and retirement ceremonies of a vice admiral, who was being replaced by a rear admiral.

Remy had invited Beau to the program. When he met Remy and me on the ship's deck, he looked handsome, even dignified, in his new grey suit.

During the ceremony, Navy personnel, clad in paper-crisp white uniforms, stood at attention. They wore tropical white uniforms, with decorations on their chests and scrambled eggs across the visors of officer's hats.

The outgoing admiral, who had 38 years of Navy service, was from an old New Orleans family. The keynote speaker was a retired U.S. Representative, also from a distinguished New Orleans family. In fact, a city hospital had been named for him.

The incoming admiral, Remy's new boss, had served as a seaman in 1943 and worked his way up through the ranks. He earned his commercial pilot's license in 1949.

Following the ceremony, guests were led on a tour of the ship. A huge buffet was spread out on the main deck. Standing off on the side, Beau and I each balanced a plate of snacks and a cup of punch in our hands.

"Remy sure is popular," said Beau, as he watched Remy being hugged by three admirals and assorted officers with whom she worked daily.

"Yes. Did you know Remy was chosen Secretary of the Year five times during her years at the Facility?"

"That's great. But why all the hugging?" Beau straightened his jacket lapels.

"It's New Orleans. You should be used to that. Everyone likes Remy. Besides, she's worked for the vice admiral for almost ten years. What's the matter, Beau, are you jealous?"

"*Non*." Beau shrugged but gave Remy the evil eye. "Guess I'm a fool to care, *je suis bete pour t'aimer.*"

Remy was used to being friendly with everyone, and she especially liked hugging male friends. Sometimes wives looked askance at her long embraces, but shrugged them off. "That's our Remy," they'd say.

Beau couldn't stand all the attention being bestowed on Remy, so he walked over to rescue her from the officers' clutches. He put his arm under her left elbow. She protested mildly, saying that she hadn't talked to everyone yet, but Beau steered her up the elevator and off the ship.

Watching them, I wondered how long Remy could put up with a jealous escort like Bayou Beau, as her friends called him behind her back.

Later that month, Angela invited Remy, Ellen, and me to take a plantation tour with the Rex Rampart's Wives' Club.

Alex drove Ellen to Remy's apartment, then we picked up Angela and drove to the drummer's house in Metairie. The bus was waiting for us when we arrived at 9 a.m. We joined club members and their guests on the coach. Angela introduced Ellen and me to the women. Some of the wives already knew Remy because she visited the club frequently with Angela.

As we headed west out of New Orleans, along the Great River Road, one of the women dispensed drinks. The rear seats of the bus were piled with coolers stocked with martini and Bloody Mary makings, wine, beer, crackers, cheese, and chips. The wives knew how to do things first-class.

Angela had been a member of the wives' group since she and Vince had sold their business and he began working at Rex Rampart's bar. The wives were close friends. They had many "nights out," or in this case a day out, where no husbands or boyfriends were allowed, except the male driver. They gossiped with the easy comfort of old friends, and their talk usually got around to their musician husbands.

"Tom's out so much, as is every member of the band, I often wonder whether he's fooling around. Do you ever think about that?" the drummer's wife asked the guitarist's wife.

"Sometimes, but I'm sure Hank is faithful. If not, as long as I don't know about it, I guess I don't worry. But...."

"Not me," Angela interrupted. "I care. If I ever find out Vince is having an affair, he'll wish he'd never been born. I swear I'll kill him and his lover."

"That's pretty rough, Angela. You couldn't shoot anybody, could you?" asked Remy.

"Don't test me," Angela snarled, her lips stretched as tight as a barbed-wire fence.

"Oooh," Ellen sighed.

Angela turned to Remy. "You're as quiet as the bayou."

"I was thinking how lucky you are to have a man like Vince. You have a long solid marriage. I thought mine would be too. It ended too soon."

"Guess I am lucky, but Vince and I have had our bad times, our ups and downs," Angela cackled. "We Italians stick together. Family means everything. It's our way."

"Beau's getting serious. I don't know if he's right for me. He's a couple of years younger than me, but I haven't told him my age. Please don't tell him."

"Our lips are sealed," Angela, Ellen, and I said in unison.

"Don't worry about age," I said. "Remember what Liz Taylor

said when she married her last husband, the young one she met at the Betty Ford Clinic? When friends asked Liz how she'd stand all that young sex, she answered, if he dies, he dies."

The women laughed.

"I don't know how you can be serious about marrying Bayou Beau...," said Ellen

Remy interrupted. "Who?"

"Sorry, that slipped out. That's what we call him."

"It's kind of cute."

"Anyway, he's not worldly. Not like Dan."

"Beauty is in the glands of the beholder." Angela cracked up at her own pun.

"But do you know how few stable, single, and straight guys there are in this city?" Remy asked. "Not to mention husband material. You can count them on one hand. One hand!"

"Oooh."

"Dan used to say that marriage, like death, is nothing to worry about," said Remy.

"Don't hurry," Ellen urged. "You've got plenty of time to decide. He's the first man who's been seriously interested in you since Dan died. There are plenty of fish in the sea."

We rode past Creole cottages, centuries-old cemeteries, and ferry boats moored along the Mississippi. This was the home of Andouille sausage, the spicy, smoked local speciality handed down from 18th and 19th century ancestors.

We pulled up in front of the San Francisco Plantation in Reserve, Louisiana. This galleried home was built in 1856 in the old Creole style, with fine decorative ceilings, false wood graining, and marbling. It was a National Historic Landmark.

The next stop was the Houmas House Plantation in Darrow. Built in 1840 as a magnificent Greek Revival mansion, it was restored in 1940 and furnished with period antiques. Formal gardens surrounded the house, and the tour guides wore antebellum costumes.

The bus driver backtracked and crossed the Mississippi, then turned west to White Castle. The group had reservations for lunch at Nottoway Plantation, the largest plantation home in the south. Also called the White Castle of Louisiana, the mansion was a blend of Greek and Italian architecture, built in 1859. This National Historic Landmark has 64 rooms, 200 windows, and 165 doors.

We gathered in the spacious Randolph Hall restaurant of Nottoway and chattered about the museum-quality antiques throughout the house. The antebellum rooms, all with private baths, had been renovated luxuriously. Guests who spend the night enjoy Plantation Breakfasts of Creole coffee and sweet potato muffins.

For lunch, most of the women selected one of the Southern or Cajun specialties on the menu. Grits and shrimp remoulade salads were served with all entrees.

"Do you know what grits means?" one of the wives asked me.

"Isn't it a sort of corn mush?"

"Girls raised in the South."

"That lets me out." I smiled.

Dessert was Randolph Hall's speciality, a fudge souffle rich with fine melted chocolate, clouds of egg whites, and hints of sugar and vanilla. I was tempted to dip my fingers in the perfectly executed dish and lick them clean, but I didn't want to embarrass my friends.

After lunch, we walked around the grounds, beneath 100-year-old oak and pecan trees and around two pools. Nottoway's 37-acre grounds overlooked the Mississippi River.

Heading back towards New Orleans, we stopped at the Oak Alley Plantation in Vacherie. Built in 1837-39 by Jacques T. Roman, this mansion is of Greek Revival architecture.

"This is my favorite plantation," said Angela as we strode towards the house under a spectacular "alley" of 28 evenly spaced live oak trees, believed to be at least 100 years older than the big house.

Our last stop was the elegant Destrehan Plantation. Built in 1787 in French Colonial style and remodeled to Greek Revival around 1830; it is the oldest documented plantation in the Lower Mississippi Valley and is listed on the National Register of Historic Places. It has hand-hewn cypress timbers, pegged attic, and bousillage, the West Indies-style hip roof. The plantation home reminded me of a picture I once saw of Robert Louis Stevenson's home in Samoa.

The hostess told us about the ghosts that began appearing in the manor house after it was restored. There was one apparition that frequently appeared—a white figure sitting in a phantom chair, crossing a driveway, or peering out a second-floor window. The spirit was thought to be Stephen Handerson, who lived in the manor with his wife, Elenore, in the 1850s. Elenore died at age 19 and Stephen, overcome by grief, died a few years later. Others say the ghost was Jean LaFitte, who owned ten pirate ships in the early 1800s. His treasure was supposedly lost nearby.

"Why, Angela, you're as white as a ghost," Remy said as we boarded the bus.

Angela grimaced. "I can feel the spirits here. I know when they're around."

At the West Bank Expressway cloverleaf, the bus turned left to cross the Huey P. Long Bridge. The old bridge was scary. It was high and its two lanes in each direction were narrow. Railroad tracks separated inbound and outbound traffic and there were missing bars in the railing. Below, barges plying the Mississippi looked like toys.

We arrived back in East New Orleans late that day, tired, but glad we had taken the trip back through the early times of Louisiana.

On Christmas Eve, Vince and Angela invited Remy, Beau, and me to their house to celebrate Reveillon, a Cajun supper held after midnight Mass. Two of the Santorini's daughters and their families were also there.

On both sides of the entry to their house stood two, fully lit, ten-foot-tall Nutcracker soldiers. Inside, Angela had decorated a tree with gold angels, cranberry-colored ribbons, beads of gold and cranberry, and twinkle lights. She had draped garlands of silk magnolia blos-soms, accented with red satin and metallic gold fabric bows on the parlor archway and over each doorway. Papier-mache figures of toy soldiers, angels, and Santa Clauses adorned tabletops.

The dining room table was set with a cranberry-colored cloth with gold brocade napkins. Ivy plants hung low over the table as a centerpiece. A buffet was spread out with platters of smoked ham, baked fish, glazed roast duck with rice dressing, baked sweet pota-toes with pineapple and mandarin orange slices, buttery brussels sprouts, pickled watermelon, and colorful maque choux, a dish of hominy, corn, and tomatoes.

"You outdid yourself, Angela," said Remy.

"Amen. Your house looks fit for a centerfold in *Gourmet* magazine," I said.

"It's nothing. I love Christmas. And I like to cook. It makes me calm. It helps me figure out my problems, especially when I'm kneading bread or cooking jambalaya."

With a mischievous twinkle in his eyes, Beau told me that Santa arrives in New Orleans on a skiff pulled through the swamp by eight alligators. Santa's a fat little drover with a long poling stick and wearing muskrat from head to foot, he added. "I'll take you and Remy to see the fireworks on the levees before the holiday season is over."

The women always exchanged Christmas presents. I was amazed at the expensive gifts, as if each one tried to outdo the other. Remy gave Ellen a rare China plate to add to her collection; Remy re-ceived a beautiful porcelain figurine of a clown from Angela; Remy gave Angela a pair of gold and pearl earrings; and they gave me an etching on black velvet of the Mississippi River curving around New Orleans.

On New Year's Eve, I invited Remy, Beau, Angela, and Vince to my apartment to celebrate. I also invited Ellen and Alex, but they didn't want to drive from Slidell on a holiday eve. I didn't blame them.

I decided to cook a Chinese dinner, slightly Americanized. I had made authentic Chinese dishes while I lived in Guam, but that took days of preparation. This time the only thing I had to do ahead of time was bake the Chinese Almond Cookies, rich with sugar, butter, egg, and almonds. I made Chinese Walnut Chicken with sherry, steamed rice, sauteed asparagus, cucumbers in sesame seeds, and gingered peaches.

"Why do you hide your culinary talents?" Remy asked me.

I laughed. "As my ex-husband used to say, 'you're a good cook—when you're in the mood.' That's so true. I have to be in a cooking mood."

I had bought a case of champagne, and we all ate and drank like pigs.

"Here's to the New year." We raised our flutes and toasted and clinked them together. We were a happy, close group. Life seemed to be going swimmingly.

Remy was sleeping frequently at Beau's house. She drove so often between her apartment and the Rigolets that her favorite song became, "On the Road Again." She would drive to the bayou in the middle of the night to make up with Beau after one of their frequent fights.

Many a Monday morning when Remy picked me up for work, her eyes would be red and she would be yawning after driving to Beau's during the night, then coming back to town to go to work. I often wondered how Remy could get by with such little sleep.

Although Remy and Beau were serious about each other, Remy told me she was still debating whether to go steady with Beau or continue playing the field. I wondered how long their relationship would last.

In June Ellen O'Reilly retired from U.S. Civil Service. She was 65 years old. Navy Facility employees hosted a farewell dinner party for her aboard the *Desire Queen* steamboat.

Beau parked his pickup in front of Remy's apartment, then we all piled into Remy's car for the ride to the pier at the foot of Canal Street.

We boarded the boat at dusk, just as the whistle sounded and the calliope played "Lady of Spain." The engine started and the paddle wheel at the stern began to churn up water. The low, mournful blast of the horn cut through the sounds of revelry, wind, and even the calliope.

I climbed to the upper deck. On the port side of the steamboat, the sunset shimmered on the Mississippi River. To starboard, shore hands tossed the ropes to the deck crew, and the small floating palace shuddered as it crawled away from the Canal Street pier.

A cool breeze caressed my cheeks as I looked down from the deck onto the Moon Walk, the wide, paved top of the levee. On most evenings, tourists wander down to Moon Walk to sit on benches facing the river and watch the sun set over the shimmering water. Couples embrace in the shadows, as boats strung with lights like big wedding cakes sweep past the far bank of the river.

Across Jackson Square, the dark towers of Saint Louis Cathedral and a fringe of trees among the mansard roofs of the city were visible against the twilight sky. As the distance between the boat and dock grew longer, the onlookers on land became smaller.

Moving up the Mississippi River, the *Desire Queen* passed the *Natchez, John James Audubon,* and the *Cotton Blossom* sternwheelers rocking at anchor at their piers as the steamboat's wake lapped towards them. Preparing to sail, the boats were ablaze with bright lights, and jazz music wafted across the water. Steamboats were extensions of the seductive, Elysian city, whose pleasures were food and wine and music.

The *Desire Queen* headed toward the center of the wide Mississippi and moved rapidly upstream. Swells of gray water poured past the hull. Its giant paddlewheel turned hypnotically, the smokestacks gushed, and the decks shuddered. There was star-drenched darkness beyond the multicolored foredeck lights, and boats drifted by with their green and red lights flickering.

The boat turned around under the Crescent City Connection Bridge and headed downriver, where she would turn again and head back upriver, back and forth for four and a half hours. Lights on the river banks twinkled on the water as the current gently stroked the crushed rocks on the levees.

I thought how pleasant a river cruise was. For a few hours, time stopped, taking passengers back to when cotton was king and life was as slow and graceful as the currents of the Mississippi. The history of the South was written along these riverbanks. The commerce of the world passes through the port of New Orleans. Cotton in bygone days. Today tobacco, whiskey, hemp, and furs from America's heartland are barged downriver to be loaded onto freighters and tankers waiting at concrete piers.

I went below to the main salon, where Ellen and Alex were seated at the head table with Navy officials. White linen cloths covered tables set with gleaming crystal and sparkling silver.

Remy and Beau had saved me a seat at their table. Dressed in his Sunday best suit, Beau's Cajun charm captivated everyone. Remy wore a flowing, full-skirted tangerine dance dress and sandals to match.

We were all eager to sample the buffet dinner spread out on side tables of the salon. The aroma of rich food, arranged like a Japanese painting, drew everyone close. At one end of the buffet were turtle soup, oysters on the half shell, and a tossed salad. In the center were chicken jambalaya, French bread, and bread pudding. A full bar was set up at the other end.

After dinner, Ellen's commander made a brief speech in which he told her how much he and everyone at the Facility would miss her. He presented her with a Navy plaque, a check from employees, and a certificate of retirement for 40 years of government service. Ellen then opened numerous gifts from others at the party.

On the upper deck, the Dukes of Dixieland band was warming up to top off the ingredients for a romantic evening. The riverboat was full to capacity, and most of the Navy group, including Remy, Beau, and myself, packed the dance floor. Couples were jitterbugging to "Rollin' On the River." I danced first with an accounting clerk and then a Navy Chief from the Facility.

It was almost dark and the temperature was falling quickly, as it often does on the river. Lights blinked on the skyline, and the river was discernible only as a wide dark band lined by lights on both levees. An empty barge chugged upstream. The ring of boats around the riverboat began to disappear. Running lights on and sails down, the long-distance racers, glided into the harbor, sleek as ghosts in the dark. On the black water, ships passed back and forth in the night. The blue lights of squad cars and patrol wagons glowed fitfully on the distant shores.

It was a gorgeous, take-your-breath-away evening. The sky sparkled with stars, and the great river flowed below. Songs were written about nights like this.

I walked around the deck and spotted Remy and Beau sitting on deck chairs in the stern. I walked up behind them, but they didn't see me. They were intent on each other, their heads together. Beau appeared to be reaching for something in his coat pocket. I overheard him say, "Remy, I know I can't give you the things Dan did, you know, diamonds and things. But I love you. I'm sure I can make you happy. Will you marry me?"

The proposal surprised me, but I guess I should have seen it coming. Remy seemed to thrive on Beau's companionship. I hurriedly tiptoed down the ladder to the main salon, where the Navy group had gathered, preparing to disembark near the main gangway.

Soon Remy and Beau entered. Beau stood in the center of the salon. "Attention y'all. I'd like to make an announcement before you leave. I don't want to take anything away from Ellen's retirement party, well deserved as y'all know it is, but I want to announce that Remy has agreed to marry me."

"Oooh." Ellen applauded along with the crowd.

"That's wonderful," said Alex. "As the Irish say, an empty bed is a widow's death."

I went outside and leaned on the deck railing as the boat neared the Canal Street pier. The sky glowed green over New Orleans on one side and Algiers on the other. A tanker passing by sounded its wail of a whistle. A small tender chugged in towards the wharf from a freighter moored in deeper water, and its running lights looked like low shooting stars in the dark.

The steam calliope played "Auld Lang Syne," as passengers walked down the gangplank and disappeared into the city.

As Remy and I waited for Beau to bring her car around from the parking lot, she whispered to me, "I'm not sure I'm doing the right thing."

"What do you mean?"

"By agreeing to marry Beau."

When Beau returned with Remy's car, she said loud enough for him to hear, "Everything's coming up roses, at last."

I smiled. How long would the roses bloom? Like fudge souffle, life can collapse. You think you have it all together. Then, bam!

CHAPTER EIGHT

In February, Remy and Beau and the Santorinis invited me to watch the Mardi Gras parade the local way, from the neutral ground uptown on St. Charles Avenue. Vince and Angela assured me this would give me a different perspective of Mardi Gras than two years ago, when Ye Olde Spaghetti House was our comfortable base. Of course, Dan was with us then.

Early on Fat Tuesday morning, Beau, 'Tit Gard, and Remy picked me up in Beau's truck. A plastic alligator dangled from the rear-view mirror on the windshield. Since the morning was warm, we all wore jeans and T-shirts, but we tossed jackets in the back of the truck in case of rain.

Remy sat between Beau and me in the front seat of the cab, while 'Tit Gard sat behind in the truck bed and peered through the rear window. Remy whispered to me she was glad she couldn't hear 'Tit Gard's whining because he was stuck in the back and not sitting up front beside his father.

Vince and Angela followed us in their car. We both drove west on I-10 and turned off at the Loyola exit to St. Charles Avenue. We were heading to the girls' school where Beau worked, so we could park our vehicles in the school grounds. On-street parking was prohibited two hours before and after a Mardi Gras parade. Cars parked in the wrong places were ticketed and sometimes towed. Also, we would be able to use the restrooms inside the school. Having access to a restroom on Fat Tuesday was a luxury.

Carrying blankets and a folding chair each, Remy, Angela, and I walked two blocks to St. Charles Avenue. Vince, Beau, and 'Tit Gard made two trips to carry more chairs and coolers full of food, beer, sodas, and a pitcher of martinis.

We spread blankets and set up chairs in a spot shaded by huge oaks on the thick green grass of the neutral ground in the center of St. Charles Avenue.

"This sure beats paying $8 each to sit in the grandstands along St. Charles." Beau handed Vince a beer.

"Beau, thanks for letting us use the school's restrooms," I said. "If I drink many beers, I'll be walking back and forth all day."

He winked. "How could I let my favorite people suffer? I can't cross my legs all day long, can you?"

Residents, rubbing sleep from their eyes, tumbled out of their columned mansions, surrounded by trimmed velvety lawns and colorful gardens. These people and other spectators lined the sidewalks and neutral grounds along the parade route, as they have been doing for the past one hundred Mardi Gras parades. Some people sat on chairs, some climbed trees or utility poles to get a good view of the parade. Others leaned against ladders, which the children would climb when the floats passed by.

Around 8:30, we heard the drums—boom, boom, boom—and the parade began. The frenzied bacchantes along the sidewalks and neutral ground went wild.

Over the din, Angela shouted, "The real point of Mardi Gras is to welcome in Lent, though it seems that no one remembers, except a rare priest or nun. In the early years of this century, Lundi Gras was celebrated on Monday when the King of Carnival arrived by boat from the Mississippi River."

"Here comes the foist float." Vince stood up to watch as the Zulu float neared.

When Rex's float passed by, the crowd cheered and screamed. The King sat on a large throne, high and ornate and splendidly decorated. He wore a jeweled crown, mask, and a long curly wig. Clad in a velvet gown, he waved his golden cup at the crowd.

Soon a high school band marched along playing the carnival theme song, "If Ever I Cease to Love." I caught the words this time: "If ever I cease to love, if ever I cease to love, may oysters have legs and cows lay eggs, if ever I cease to love."

Next came the floats of Argus and Comus, with torches ablaze and brass bands playing savage rhythms. The mammoth structures, rolling slowly down the avenue, towered above the heads of the jubilant crowds. People surged into the street as, from atop quivering papier-mache floats, men in glittering satin costumes and masks threw glass necklaces, wooden beads, doubloons, and plastic cups to them. I caught my share of throws.

The parade proceeded up St. Charles Avenue, around Lee Circle, and toward Canal Street on the edge of the French Quarter. I could picture the locals at Lee Circle. Surrounded by bags of po'boys and beer, they'd sit on the steps beneath the equestrian statue of Robert E. Lee, carved from Tennessee marble.

Around noon, Beau said, "Hey, y'all, I'm hungry."

Angela and Remy took containers from the coolers and spread them out on a blanket. We gathered around to help ourselves to muffalettas, crab gumbo, deviled eggs, Mardi Gras salad and rice, as well as chips, crackers, dip, deviled eggs, and pralines.

"What a picnic!" I savored a mouthful of gumbo. "I'd like to go to a Mardi Gras ball, just once."

Vince nodded. "We went years ago. It's hard to get invited these days, unless you're members of a krewe or a VIP."

"One year Dan and I were invited to the Twelfth Night Revelers Carnival Ball at the opera house," Remy said. "I still have a musical jewelry box inscribed with the name of the krewe and date of the ball."

"Used to be that if a man reigned as king, or his daughter was named queen of a krewe, his social status and business standing soared," said Beau.

"In the past," Vince added, "decent women weren't allowed to take part in carnival parades. People thought women who wore masks and costumes were loose and lacked morals."

Angela cackled, "Nowadays there are all-female krewes, mixed-sex krewes, and family-oriented and truck-parade krewes."

Late afternoon, Angela unveiled her home-made King Cake, an oval, braided coffee cake topped with cinnamon sugar in Mardi Gras colors—gold, green, and purple. Hidden in the cake was a tiny plastic baby doll, which had replaced the coin used in the cakes during medieval times. Traditionally, the person who finds the doll is crowned king or queen and has to buy the next cake or host the next party.

"The custom," Angela explained, "is to give King Cakes to family and friends between January 6, the Feast of the Epiphany, and Mardi Gras. About 750,000 King Cakes are eaten during Carnival season, can you believe that? We give presents to children during this period. This custom started with the Three Wise Men, who followed a star and gave gifts to the Christ child."

Beau sliced a piece of cake and offered a bite to Remy. "Open up, *cherie.*"

We didn't eat the entire King Cake, and none of us found the doll. One of Angela's children or grandchildren would probably have that honor when they ate the remainder of the cake.

By 5 p.m., when the Elks Jefferson, Elks Orleans, and Crescent City truck krewes sped by, we knew the parade was over. We gathered our belongings and trash and carried them back to our vehicles. Soon there remained only the beaten-down grass of the neutral ground, littered from the day-long mayhem.

On the way home, Beau commented, "Well, that's the last big party until St. Patrick's Day."

"You wouldn't believe how many heads of cabbage are tossed from floats during the St. Patrick's Day parade," Angela said. "And bread altars are baked to celebrate St. Joseph's day next. That's an Italian tradition."

"Then comes the JazzFest," said Remy. "That's a big event too."

"Where's that held?"

"At the fairgrounds. But it's usually so rainy and muddy that

I've never gone to one. It's a mess," said Remy. "It's N'awlins' answer to the Grand Ole Opry."

Months before Easter, Angela had made reservations for us four women for Sunday brunch at Antoine's, in the French Quarter.

When Lent officially ended at Easter, the mood seemed to change overnight. Good Friday was gray and chilly, yet Easter Sunday dawned bright as a sequin. That morning, Remy parked in Dan's favorite parking garage, and we walked the few blocks to Antoine's. Along the way, we watched the first of four parades proceeding along Bourbon Street toward Jackson Square.

"I feel naked without an Easter bonnet," I said. Remy and I were bareheaded, but Angela and Ellen wore their best Sunday-go-to-church hats.

"Oooh. Look at those hats." Ellen pointed to a caravan of horse-drawn carriages traveling down Bourbon Street. The women were sporting colorful hats as they made their way to the St. Louis Cathedral to attend Mass.

"Here comes another parade." I turned to see women wearing peach and purple hats and gowns.

"They're called Friends of Germaine Wells," Ellen said. "She was the daughter of Count Arnaud and the late owner of the restaurant bearing his name. After their hats are judged, they go to Arnaud's for Bloody Marys."

"Germaine was no lady," said Angela. "And her male friends weren't exactly the city's finest." She waved to two of her friends she had met during her years in the Quarter. "Here comes my favorite."

Organized by Mrs. Chris Owens, a Bourbon Street club owner and dancer, this parade featured women riding in carriages and cars bedecked with pastel balloons. The women wore eye-popping hats dripping with chiffon veils or bunny ears.

"Hey, I caught some beads," I said and hung them around my neck.

"Here comes the raunchiest parade of them all," said Remy. A dozen drag queens wearing huge hats sauntered on high heels between saloons on Bourbon Street.

"What a sight!" I said. "Only in New Orleans."

Arriving at Antoine's, we were seated at a table, set with elegant crystal, china, and silverware.

After a lunch of Oysters Rockefeller, Remy said, "Here comes the pyrotechnics."

I was puzzled until I saw our waiter preparing cups of Café Brulot. A blue flame cascaded from a large silver bowl as the waiter ladled the fragrant steaming liquid into our cups.

We all selected Cherries Jubilee for dessert. More pyrotechnics. The waiter poured a cup of brandy into a silver bowl containing large dark cherries. Then he ignited the brandy and stirred the mixture with a silver ladle. Blue flames leaped and danced until the juices of the simmering cherries were thoroughly blended with the seething spirits. All that was spooned over domes of ice cream. It was sinful. My taste buds had an orgasm.

Just as Easter signaled resurrection, Remy felt renewed, looking forward to what was to come. Yesterday was so different, she said. Today she was in another world where birds sang more gaily, grass glistened with globules of morning dew, and flowers were more colorful and fragrant after heavy rains.

As quickly as spring had arrived, summer followed within a week. People opened windows all over the city and perspiration rolled down their cheeks and arms. The air was filled with the pleasant odors of new grass and rosebuds, and bluebirds, robins, and sparrows chittered from gutters of eaves and skittered on the rims of courtyard birdbaths.

In late June, Remy, Ellen, and I took Angela to lunch at Commander's Palace to celebrate her birthday. Remy parked a few blocks away from the restaurant, located in the heart of the Garden District.

The 25-city-block Garden District is bordered by Jackson and Louisiana Avenues, between St. Charles Avenue and Magazine Street.

The District lives up to its name. In summer, pink, salmon, and fuchsia azaleas are ablaze alongside the streetcar tracks in the neutral ground and grow in thick banks against the mansions that line the street. Dark green lawns around houses are edged with white impatiens. Crape myrtles in every shade of pink and purple grow in rows between houses, and huge oaks spread their umbrellas high above the avenue, lending a cool, green shade to all galleries. Magnolias like white faces and shiny dark leaves stare from the shadows. Luxuriant bougainvillea vines tumble off roofs, and sweet olive trees fill the air with a soft perfume.

"I'm glad we're early so we can go through the cemetery," said Angela. "I haven't visited my mother's grave in a year."

"Did I tell you that my great-grandmother was buried here?" I said.

"No kidding? Small world, eh?"

"My mother's been delving into genealogy lately. She learned that her father was born in New Orleans in 1884. His mother had also been born in New Orleans in 1850, and, in 1925, she was buried here in Lafayette No. 1 Cemetery. I checked at the Historic Collection of New Orleans in the Quarter and discovered that St. Alphonse, the church where her funeral was held, is no longer standing. Its records were destroyed too."

"Maybe we can find her grave," said Remy.

"I hope so, but the researcher said that many graves have been either vandalized or eroded by the weather."

On the short walk to the cemetery, I began humming the bouncy tune, "Way Down Yonder in New Orleans."

"You sound happy," said Remy.

I smiled. "I was thinking of my mother. She told me that her father used to sing this song as he danced with me on his shoulders around our livingroom."

Under archways of oak branches, we stepped carefully on the uneven cobblestone sidewalks covered with fallen magnolia leaves. The pavement at each intersection was embedded with ceramic tiles that spelled out the street name.

We passed a house where a skull and crossbones had been discovered under the floorboards during renovation. Owners believed they were voodoo relics hidden long ago by servants. Another house nearby was built by slaves and owned by a friend of Jefferson Davis, the President of the Confederacy. Davis died in one of the rooms in 1889.

"Isn't this close to Anne Rice's house?" I asked.

"I think so," said Remy.

"Fitting, isn't it, that she lives near a cemetery while writing about witches and vampires?"

As we approached the corner of Prytania Street and Washington Avenue, Ellen said that this cemetery was once part of a plantation owned by Bienville, the founder of New Orleans. It was laid out in 1883, and within twenty years, it was filled with many Irish and German victims of the 1895 yellow fever epidemic that devastated the city's population.

We walked under the arched iron gates into the cemetery, called the Walled City of the Dead. We stepped along the narrow concrete walkways, overgrown with grass, and stood on tiptoes to see over the rows of high tombs, the above-ground structures similar to miniature houses. The dead were buried above ground because of the marshy soil in which graves often filled with water before they could be closed. A body of architecture evolved to produce the myriad shapes of vaults, obelisks, and monuments that dominate the cemetery's skyline, resembling a small city. Some family plots, with crypts of carved portals and moldering vaults, were enclosed by iron fences.

There were heaps of withering flowers on some tombs, and, on others, marble vases had been cemented to the front step to hold fresh-cut flowers. Decorations on pink marble gravestones ranged from sleeping lambs and angels sitting atop children's stones and open Bibles to bouquets of flowers carved on square blocks.

I read the inscriptions on each tombstone I passed, hoping to find my great-grandmother's grave. "What's this?" I stepped around a pile of dry yellowed pieces of something lying on the ground.

Ellen and Remy came over to look. "Looks like bones."

"Yuk." The bones were plainly visible around graves that had either been vandalized or badly weathered with age.

Angela found the grave of her aunt, who was buried there in the early 1920s. Although chunks of the marble marker had been broken off, some of the inscription on the gravestone remained: "...She was a good mother, good friend, and mourned by all who knew her. *Passants priez pour elle.*" Angela made the sign of the cross and turned away.

"Cemeteries are kind of friendly. You can almost imagine you're at home with your ancestors," I said. "Wish I could find my great-grandmother's grave."

"Guess something happened to it. That's too bad," said Remy.

Angela ran her fingers over a smooth marble statue of an angel atop one of the gravestones. "I still remember my eighth grade teacher, a Catholic nun with an Irish brogue. She liked to tell us tales about witches and the Irish Ghost who haunted the Garden District. She was brutal. I'll never forget her steely fingers gripping my arm, or the way she smacked our knuckles with rulers when we disobeyed her. Speaking of witches," she continued, "have any of you seen the chicken man while you were cruising in the Quarter?"

None of us had seen him.

"I used to see him when Vince and I owned Evangeline's Desire Bar. He was a poor, gentle guy who carried a walking cane and a bag of magic potion called gris gris. He'd bite off the heads of chickens during rituals. The French Quarter was his church. He gave everything away to anybody, gay or straight, young or old. He died recently and he was given a voodoo funeral with a jazz band and bongo drummers. He's on the other side now, like Marie Laveau, the voodoo queen."

New Orleans is called a haunted city, a ghostly city that festers with secrets in the perpetual Carribean heat. Voodoo, or hoodoo as it's sometimes spelled, rituals provide an unobstructed view of history, in which 300 years of America pass like the mist of morning. The cities of the dead stand as symbols of a culture that accepts the sorrows along with the joys of life. They're pure New Orleans. I felt as if I was suspended somewhere between the physical and spiritual worlds.

As we were leaving the cemetery, a busload of tourists parked at the curb. The visitors, cameras ready, scrambled out of the bus to visit the cemetery.

We crossed the street to Commander's Palace. Before we entered the small foyer, Angela remarked that the restaurant was called the dead center of the Garden District.

"Oooh."

Commander's Palace, built by Emile Commander in 1880, has served as a private residence, a restaurant, and a Prohibition-era bordello. Ella and Dick Brennan took over the rambling mansion in the early 1970s, restored it, and furnished it with Victorian antiques. It became New Orleans' five-star restaurant. The neighborhood was shocked when the Brennans had the house repainted white and aquamarine, but it's now a famous landmark.

One of the Brennan family is always on duty to oversee meals. Ella Brennan says, with a wry Irish smile, "Food in New Orleans is like sex; everybody's interested."

What a contrast after walking through the cemetery with its decaying tombs, I thought, as the waiter showed us to an elegantly appointed table in one of the brightly decorated upstairs dining rooms.

The menu offered classic Creole inventions: Ramos gin fizzes; rounds of buttered and toasted French bread flavored with cheese and garlic; thick and meaty turtle soup; fresh shrimp in a pungent remoulade; eggs Creole, eggs Sardou, and eggs Hussarde; chicory flavored coffee; and Creole bread-pudding souffle.

We all ordered soup du jour or confit of game salad, then I ordered wood-fired Gulf fish, Angela selected tenderloin of beef tips, Remy the Commander's mixed grill, and Ellen soft shell crab salad. We topped off the delicious lunch with Creole bread pudding, its hot center cooled by whiskey custard.

"I'd like to bottle this, " I said, breathing deeply of the heavenly aroma. "And look how beautifully all the dishes are presented—picture-perfect."

When Angela left the table to go to the ladies' room, I said, "Angela seems to have a sixth sense about ghosts. Remember how she shivered when we heard about the ghosts at the Destrehan Plantation when we were on the Rex Rampart's wives' tour? Does she practice voodoo?"

"Angela?" Remy shrugged her shoulders. "Well, she does have voodoo charms, a few candles that represent...."

"Oooh. That's black-magic stuff," Ellen interrupted.

"I think she goes beyond trinkets and costume jewelry," said Remy. "I've seen a voodoo doll, an effigy of a woman in her altar room, actually a walk-in closet. The walls are decorated with African masks, metal carvings, and statues of Christian saints. There are candles, sticks of incense, and ju-ju, the bones and skulls of animals. In one corner a wooden snake curls around a crucifix. She believes that unguents and potions can cure sickness or help lovers, and she knows what powder to use or what candle to burn to counteract a spell or to command the spirits."

"That's hard to believe," I said. "Angela acts so saintly, like an angel. And she always wears a gold cross around her neck."

Ellen said Angela had been brought up in a strict Italian Catholic family, but, like some Catholics in New Orleans, she had become Creolized. They adapted their religion to fit their sense of spirituality.

Angela returned to the table as a trio of jazz musicians strolled among the tables and played a Louis Armstrong favorite, "What a Wonderful World."

"It certainly is a wonderful world here," I said.

"Happy birthday, Angela." We toasted.

"Many, many more happy years," I said. "You know, someday Ellen will be 70 years old, Remy will be 65, I'll be 55, and Angela will keep telling us she's 45."

Still laughing, we paid the check and left the restaurant.

CHAPTER NINE

On a summer Saturday, glorious with a robin's-egg-blue sky and low humidity, Remy and I drove along St. Charles Avenue, which tunneled through a long green-black corridor of moss-hung oak trees, swirling with mist. No one hurried through the Garden District. Traffic moved at a decorous pace. St. Charles Avenue was never quiet. Besides the many automobiles that travel up and down the narrow lanes, the peeling green-painted wooden streetcars, with red-bordered windows, clanged and rattled up and down the neutral ground like San Francisco cable cars.

Remy turned left off St. Charles Avenue towards the river to the Audubon Zoo, of which both of us were members. Close to the zoo entrance were the magnificent buildings that once housed the Louisiana Cotton Centennial exposition.

While strolling around the zoo, Remy pointed out the highest spot in New Orleans, not counting highway overpasses. "That's Monkey Hill. It was built so children who have never left the city could see what a hill was."

We ate lunch at the Pontchartrain Hotel's Caribbean Room, with candlelight, white tablecloths, waiters who looked like ghosts or vampires with black jackets and stiff white shirts.

"Beau's got such a big ego," Remy said. "He told me once, you've got me, lucky girl. I feel sorry for other women—only one can have me as a husband. You're holding the winning hand—mine. You're the girl with everything—me."

"Yeah, that's some ego all right."

"I'm not sure I can live out there in the Rigolets. I'd have to drive so far to work every day. And when I retire, could I sit at home and watch the fishermen motoring up and down the bayou or gossip with housewives? And you can't get away from the odor of seaweed and fish," Remy admitted.

"But, you know, Remy," I said, "I think Dan would approve of Beau."

"Maybe so. For some reason, he felt akin to the Cajuns."

"Dan, like Beau, relished good food, good times."

"You could be right," Remy smiled. "I never thought of that. I like to have a man around. It's no fun sleeping alone. Beau's so cute. He closes his eyes when he kisses and he has a big tongue."

I was surprised to learn such intimate details, but Remy and I could tell each other anything. Nothing shocked us, and we didn't make judgments. "Well, they say that the bigger a man's tongue is, the larger his equipment is. Or the bigger his heart is."

Remy blushed. "Well, that's true in Beau's case. Don't tell him I told you that. His heart's big too."

"I couldn't say that about my last husband. His tongue was big, but his doo-dah was puny. And he didn't have a heart."

"Someday," I continued, "I'd like to ride the St. Charles trolley to the end of the line."

"That's Riverbend, where the streetcars turn around. It's a unique section of N'awlins. It's here that the meandering Mississippi shapes the city, and cradles it into the upper horn of a crescent. That's where its nickname, the Crescent City, came from," explained Remy. "It's a university area full of coffeehouses, art galleries, bookstores, flower shops, juice bars, and vegetarian restaurants. There's not much litter there and hardly any graffiti."

Later that month, Remy and Beau flew to upstate New York. Remy wanted to introduce Beau to her mother. While they were gone, I stopped by Remy's apartment every afternoon after work to take care of Pooh.

When I'd enter the foyer, Pooh would greet me and follow me into the kitchen. Pooh wasn't too fond of cat food. She preferred a can of red salmon, smoked oysters, or turkey and chicken. Remy always left bowls of water and dry food for Pooh, but she'd kill for liver. Before Remy left on her trip, she boiled liver and put it in the freezer so I'd have a supply of Pooh's favorite meal. As I cut the liver into bite-size pieces and mixed it with a small amount of canned food, Pooh would wash her paws and whiskers, as if she were a child washing up before dinner. Within seconds, the liver was gone.

I was a dog lover. I had never been fond of cats, but I'd sit with Pooh for a while so she wouldn't get too lonely. She would approach me slowly to be admired. I crouched down and gave her an afternoon's dose of affection. Of course, she kept her back to me, pretending that she didn't know me. Even if she thought I existed, it would have been a matter of perfect indifference to her.

When I sat on the lounge in the TV room to watch the evening news, Pooh sometimes condescended to jump up on my lap, but she usually lay across the room on the daybed and purred.

When Remy returned home, she thanked me.

"You're very welcome. I enjoy being with Pooh. How was your trip?"

"Well, my mother liked Beau. It's a shame she can't live with me here. I think she'd like it, but at least she seems content in the nursing home. She's made a lot of friends there.

"Anyway, Beau and I argued about when and where the wedding should be. We argued about living on the bayou. I hate to think about the long drive to and from New Orleans. Also, Beau told me that he wants us to have a Cajun wedding. He wants us to be married in a pirogue on the water, with guests surrounding us in boats. After the ceremony, it's the custom for the bride and groom to walk around the floor in a traditional Marche des Maries. Then the newlyweds dance a waltz and invite everyone to join in. All the while, guests pin money on the bride's veil until she's wearing a headdress of money. Can you picture me doing those things? Ha! Besides, I don't intend to wear a veil. I'd rather fly to Las Vegas for a quick, simple ceremony."

"Is there even going to be a wedding?" I asked.

Remy shrugged and put her hands in the air. "Who knows?"

On a Saturday evening in July, Beau, Remy, and the O'Reillys took me to dinner to celebrate my big FIVE-O birthday. Vince had to work at Rex Rampart's club that evening, so he couldn't join us for dinner. Angela decided to stay home, but she sent me a cute birthday card.

As I walked around the lake to Remy's apartment, the sky deepened to gold and the sun set. I couldn't understand how quickly the years had flown by, and it made no sense to me at all that I was fifty, although everyone told me I didn't look my age. Whatever my appearance, I had fifty-year-old memories.

Minutes after I arrived at Remy's apartment, Beau came in and caught her in a spasmodic embrace. She nuzzled his neck. They kissed and both sighed contentedly.

"What're you makin' for dinner tonight?" Beau asked Remy.

"Reservations." Remy gave Beau her 100-watt smile. "Let's go."

When we arrived at a Cajun restaurant in Slidell, Ellen and Alex were already seated. The walls of the small room were lined with stuffed fish, ropy fishnets, seashells, starfish, old floats, and other nautical paraphernalia to create a seascape that looked like Davey Jones' locker. On the postage-stamp-size floor, people were gyrating to the clamor of a three-piece zydeco band—an accordion, stand-up bass, and mandolin. The crowd was local, but Ellen said tourists were beginning to find the place by its spreading reputation for good food.

The air was heavy with that down-home smell of mouth-watering, high cholesterol Southern fried fish.

We all ordered the speciality of the house, which was the Cajun equivalent of British fish and chips: fried catfish, French fries, cole slaw, and hush puppies.

"What did you do today?" Remy asked me. "I tried to call you this morning, but you weren't home."

"I went downtown. On the way home, I stopped by the Ford

dealer's on Chef Menteur. I bought a car."

Everyone clapped. "It's about time you had your own wheels," said Beau. "What did you get?"

"A white Ford Mustang hatchback, last year's model. It was on sale. I pick it up next Wednesday, then I'll go to the motor vehicles department to trade my Guam's driver's license for a Louisiana one."

I grinned proudly as they raised their martini glasses in a toast to me and my new car.

"Congratulations, Grace," said Ellen.

"Happy birthday."

"Thanks."

"Remember that like great wine, we get better as we get older," said Remy.

"On the other hand," said Beau, "As you get older, you feel better with lots of great wine."

"Very clever." I raised my glass to them. "Thanks for the great birthday party."

"When's the big day?" Alex relit his cigar and blew smoke between Beau and Remy.

"I'm just waitin' for Remy to make up her mind. I'm ready."

"What's holding you back?" Ellen wanted to know.

"I don't know. Guess I'm not ready yet."

"You'd better decide," said Ellen, crunching on a French fry, "before Beau slips away."

Beau winked at Ellen and squeezed her hand.

Beau and Remy saw each other every day during the weeks that followed. Those weeks could be compressed into one of those dreamy "falling in love" sequences that filled screens about halfway through most romantic movies. With symphonic music swelling in the distance, I pictured Remy and Beau dining out, dancing in the ballroom, holding hands at movies, puttering around the bayou in Beau's boat. I see their heads almost touching, carrying on intimate conversations in romantic restaurants.

I didn't see Remy as much as I used to before she and Beau

became engaged. I missed her and tried not to be jealous that Beau was taking up most of her time. She seemed to sense that and invited me to spend a Saturday night at Beau's.

That morning, I picked up Remy in my new Mustang. We had lunch and shopped at the Plaza in East New Orleans before driving to Beau's house.

When we arrived, Beau took us for a short motorboat ride, after which we came back to his house. He had invited a few of his neighbors to join us. He had caught buckets of crabs and cleaned them on the picnic table under his house. He made crab cakes bound together with flour and egg whites, then flavored with Chablis, capers, scallions, and cayenne pepper. He also served fried shrimp, hush puppies, and raw oysters. Beau could shuck an oyster in under five seconds.

Later, when Remy and I were washing dishes in the kitchen, Beau called from the livingroom: "What would you two like to do tonight? How about going to a cockfight?"

"Are cockfights legal here?" I asked. "I thought they were only legal in Guam and Puerto Rico."

"It's a big gambling thing here, as popular as horse racing and cards," Beau explained. "Here, fighting cocks are called fowl and aren't protected by animal rights laws. Guess you call it quasi-legal. Cockfights are held in outlying parishes on Saturday nights. You should see the people who show up—farmers, fishermen, truck drivers, college students, lawyers."

"I'll pass," I said. "Reminds me of the old Roman games."

"Me too. I can't stand all that blood."

"Nothing happens at cockfights that roosters don't do to themselves in barnyards," said Beau.

I snorted. "At least on the farm, the birds don't have spurs and blades on their legs."

Beau poured after dinner drinks. "Come on out for the best sunset you'll ever see."

We followed him to the back porch and sat down in cane rocking chairs that looked like they'd been salvaged from the *Ti-*

tanic. The sun's last rays of the day settled over the bayou. Birds settled in their treetop nests. All was well with the world.

Back inside, Beau asked me, "Have you ever played Cajun strip scrabble?"

"No. What's that?"

Beau explained the card game. "When a player's points reach 50, the other players have to take off a piece of clothing."

Within the hour, Beau had accumulated 150 points. Remy had forfeited her blouse and slacks, which left her wearing only bra and panties.

I stood up. I'd only lost my shoes and socks. "I think I'll fold. You two can keep on playing. I'm going to get ready for bed."

When I finished brushing my teeth and washing my face, Remy and Beau had retired to the master bedroom. I could hear Remy giggling.

Remy had made up the sofa bed for me in the livingroom. I didn't mind sleeping there, even though 'Tit Gard's bedroom was empty. He sulked if anyone even entered his room, let alone slept in his bed, Remy told me. He visited his father every other weekend, but he wanted to run his father's life. She said he didn't like the women his father had been dating after the divorce and resented Remy sleeping over.

That night I dreamed about Tommy Dorsey's hit, "Tangerine." It reminded me of Remy. "She's got the guys in a whirl, but she's only fooling one girl...."

In the morning, Beau cooked Eggs Andouille. He measured a teaspoon of salt in the palm of his hand, then added a lagniappe. He splashed Tabasco on the eggs. "Cajuns like well-seasoned food. Gotta kick it up a notch, as Emeril Lagasse says."

"Oh, does it smell good in here."

Beau winked mischievously at me.

"You're a great cook, Beau." I sipped my second cup of coffee. "You remind me of Justin Wilson."

Beau grinned. "All I need is red suspenders, eh? I learned to cook since I started baching it after 20 years of marriage. 'Tit Gard

and I eat real good out here. We love to eat, love to have fun cooking. Wine takes the bitterness out of food. And I use a lot of parsley. It freshens your breath so you don't smell so bad from all that
garlic."

After breakfast, the phone rang. Beau answered it in the
kitchen.

Remy was in the bedroom making the bed and packing her
overnite bag. When she finished and came into the livingroom,
Beau hung up the phone and walked towards her.

"Why does your ex-wife always call when I'm here?" Remy
put her hands on her hips. "Or does she call you every day?"

Beau winked. "I'm irresistible."

Remy scoffed.

"She's always hollerin' at me for letting 'Tit Gard stay here so
often. She doesn't like that one bit. She's gotten hoity-toity now
that she's got a city boyfriend. She thinks I'm a bad influence on
the boy and doesn't want him to learn my old ways."

"Why didn't you tell her you have company? She kept you on
the line talking about nothing."

"She misses me. As I said, I'm irresistible."

"If you're still crazy about her, why do you want to marry me?
How can we be happy with her butting in all the time?"

Beau turned away without saying a word.

Having already packed my overnight bag, I went out on the
back porch to scan the bayou. The door didn't shut tightly behind
me and I could hear Remy and Beau arguing inside. I compared
the couple's romance to a roller coaster, with plenty of thrills, ups
and downs, and screams.

"So you'd rather cowtow to her than be nice to me." Remy
railed. "She'll hound you forever. What kind of a marriage can we
have?"

I stepped back into the kitchen just in time to see Beau take
Remy in his arms.

Remy struggled free and slapped his face. "You don't really
love me. Go to hell, you bayou rat."

"What have I done?"

"I'm getting out of here," Remy screamed. "I never want to see you or your crooked dick again."

"I figured I'd be walking into the jaws of death when I thought about marrying a widow. You're a selfish bitch. All you care about is gold and diamonds and screwing."

"Up yours, mullet-head. I won't be back." Remy grabbed her small suitcase and headed for the front door.

"It can't be *c'est tout*. Call me later when you've cooled down. Love ya."

I went down the front steps to start the car. Then I heard a crash.

Remy ran down the stairs. "Let's go." She jumped into the car. I revved up the engine and backed out of the driveway.

"What was that crash?"

"I was so mad, I threw that ceramic paddlewheel music box at him, the one he gave me for my birthday. It missed him and broke on the porch."

As we drove away, Beau stood at the top of the stairs. He shot Remy a sharp, icy look that could have opened an oyster at fifty paces.

CHAPTER TEN

To help Remy forget about Beau, Angela and I suggested that we spend a weekend in the Florida panhandle. Remy was delighted to get away. We invited Ellen, but she declined because Alex didn't want her to go with us. Who would cook his meals, empty his ash trays, and feed the cat?

Friday evening after work, Remy and I picked up Angela. We drove east on Interstate 10, midst a steady stream of 18-wheelers rumbling by. It was a four-hour drive from New Orleans to Fort Walton Beach, Florida.

We sped along the coast of the Gulf of Mexico, with its sugar-white beaches and clear green water. Across Mississippi, the dark swampy woodlands closed in on us. We drove through little helter-skelter towns with neon signs flashing "rooms."

"If Beau was driving, he'd have a roadie in his hand," said Remy.

"What's a roadie?" I asked.

"A can of Dixie beer for the road."

"Is it legal to drink while driving in Louisiana or Mississippi?"

"Yea. We don't have a Bubba law in Louisiana," said Angela. "It's legal to drink and drive. But I'll bet it's not legal in Mississippi and Florida."

"Probably not. Remember, that's the Bible belt," said Remy. "Those people call N'awlins 'sin city.' "

"I thought 'sin city' was Las Vegas," I remarked.

We made a pit stop at the Florida Welcome Center. The counter clerk gave us each a glass of orange juice and asked us to sign the guest register. "Y'all come back 'n see us now."

We continued driving west. It was a long slow crawl out of Pensacola, with bumper to bumper cars and trucks. There was also heavy air traffic near Pensacola Naval Air Station.

Fort Walton Beach, 40 miles east of Pensacola, sprawls in the middle of an endless prairie of sand fleas, land crabs, rattlesnakes, alligators, scrub oak, pelicans, herons, eagles, and beaches. Sand dunes stand like wooden bleachers overlooking the Gulf. The dunes are covered with sea oats, which have long roots and provide support for the dunes. It's illegal to pick sea oats; they're protected by Florida law. Several large white domed structures, Air Force listening devices with ears aimed at Cuba, perch like sentinels on the beaches of the peninsula known as Santa Rosa Island.

"It's easy to see why this area is called the Emerald Coast," I said. "This looks like the Bahamas."

"Some people call this area L.A."

"Los Angeles?"

"Lower Alabama." Angela's shrill laugh spanned an octave in two notes.

"What'd I tell you?" Angela pointed to a wooden shack on the beachside of the road. The store's sign hung above the open door said, "Rowdy's Retreat." Other signs nailed to the sides of the building touted "Pork Rinds" and "Pit Bulls Welcome."

"Florida's not all Disneyland, that's for sure," I said.

As we drove across the bridge to Santa Rosa Island, we first heard, then saw, the lights of a V-shaped wedge of giant planes approaching at 1,000 feet. Squadrons of B-36s were stationed thirteen miles north of the beach town at Eglin Air Force Base, the largest in the country. In the 1950s, UFOs hovered over the panhandle's military bases, headquarters of the first pilotless B-47 drone and a proving ground where pilots are trained to drop 500-pound napalm bombs.

We checked into the Holiday Inn on Santa Rosa Island around

9 p.m. After we unpacked, we walked next door for a late dinner at a German restaurant.

"I'm sorry to hear you and Beau broke up." Angela swallowed a forkful of jagerschnitzel.

"We had another nasty fight, worse than the one Grace heard. Then I returned his engagement ring. I can't live with that nasty 'Tit Gard and Beau's ex-wife pestering me. I deserve better."

"Bayou Beau's a decent man and he loves you, but I think you could do better, too. He's not very worldly." Angela and I agreed.

"He's a Cajun rube," Remy laughed. "I hoped our affair would grow into real love, but deep down inside I think I knew it wouldn't."

Angela reminded us of the old Mississippi levee song. She sang, off-key, like a rutting gator, "The river is a rover. Do not take it for your lover, lead it to the open sea...The suitor, like a river, shifts, moving with hidden force...The river, like a suitor, will destroy you to be free...."

On Saturday morning the sun loomed like a huge psychedelic beach ball just above the horizon. The air was humid, heavy as lead, and only a seagull's screech broke the silence of the Gulf shore.

Remy dressed in a pink short-sleeved Beverly Hills Polo Club shirt with three top buttons open and skimpy white Goolagong shorts. The shorts showed off her long strong legs, shaped like a dancer's with full calves and slender ankles.

From our hotel room, Remy telephoned her long-time friends Glenda and Hank Smith, who lived in Navarre Beach, a gulfside settlement on Santa Rosa Island. Glenda invited us to come to their house for lunch. Of course, Remy accepted. She hadn't seen the couple since Dan's funeral.

As we drove west on the same coastal road we had taken from Pensacola, Remy told us that she and Dan had met the Smiths while they were all stationed in Budapest. In fact, she and her first husband knew them before Dan met them. When Hank retired as a colonel in the Air Force, the couple moved back to their home state of Florida and had a house built on the beach.

Remy turned left onto a narrow bridge that crossed the inter-coastal canal to the island. A sign welcomed us to the Gulf Islands National Seashore, an area of some 10,000 acres of protected beaches on the Gulf of Mexico. Then Remy drove west on the sandy strip of a road, passing the Holiday Inn, a mom-and-pop restaurant, a general store that sold boating and fishing equipment, and many weather-beaten homes perched on the dunes overlooking the Gulf of Mexico.

Glenda was waiting for us as Remy parked in front of her large wooden house. She hugged Remy and shook hands with Angela and me. We had all met briefly at Dan's funeral. "Come on in, Hank's fixing martinis."

We followed Glenda up steep wooden stairs, across the front deck, and into the livingroom. A glass wall faced the Gulf side of the house where a deck overlooked the water and the white sand beach.

Hank came out from behind the bar where he had been stir-ring a pitcher of martinis. He stood an inch over six feet tall and his beach shorts showed off long, muscular legs. He was a hand-some man who looked too young to be retired.

"Remy, how're you doing?" Hank gave Remy a bear hug. She clung to him for a few minutes. Tears fell down her cheeks. "Now, now." He wiped away her tears.

Hank gave each of us a martini in a chilled glass.

"I've missed you two." Remy took a sip of her martini. "You haven't lost your touch." She raised her glass to toast Hank.

"How's your social life, Remy?" Hank asked. "Keeping busy?"

"I'm fine. My friends keep me busy." Remy nodded at Angela and me. "I was engaged to a Cajun man for a while, but we broke up recently."

"That's too bad. You'll find someone else."

"Tell me about it," Remy laughed. "Grace and I go to singles dances in Metairie, but so far we haven't met anyone interesting."

"Well, you will soon. You're an attractive, intelligent woman," Glenda said as she flitted around the kitchen like a sandpiper.

"Thanks. I'll let you know!"

"Is everyone ready for lunch?" asked Glenda.

We went outside to the deck where Glenda had spread out potato salad, ham and roast beef slices, tomatoes, onions, green salad, French bread rolls, and Key Lime Pie on the long, wooden table.

"You've certainly prepared a big feast at very short notice," I said.

"When you have a beach house, you're always having guests, sometimes uninvited. I keep plenty of food on hand."

We sipped iced tea and admired the view of the Gulf of Mexico.

"This is lovely. I could sit here all day. Do the waves ever come up to the house?" I asked.

"Oh, yes. Last fall, Hurricane Nina made the Gulf boil. High waves lifted our boat up onto the beach and part of the pier was smashed. As you can see, we're having the pier repaired now. The water stopped a few feet under the pilings of the house."

"It's so peaceful. I could sit here forever, but I guess we should go," said Remy. "Thanks for your hospitality. Please don't be strangers. Come to N'awlins sometime soon. My guest room is always ready for you." She hugged Glenda, then stayed in Hank's arms for a few minutes.

After leaving the Smiths, we stopped at the beachside Holiday Inn. We strolled through the shopping arcade and stopped at an exclusive dress shop that catered to hotel guests. Remy bought a dressy tangerine-colored jumpsuit, but Angela and I didn't find anything we needed or couldn't live without.

Late that afternoon, we drove to Eglin Air Force Base for happy hour at the officers' club. Remy had a Navy Facility sticker on the bumper of her car that allowed her to enter the Marine-guarded gate.

When we walked into the club, the men stopped talking and gawked at Remy, who wore her new jumpsuit. She had a look of throwing caution to the wind and a quality that made men and women wonder if she were someone important.

"I love to watch those fly boys," said Remy as we hopped onto barstools. "Those tight flight suits show off their buns. Makes me want to reach out and grab them. Too bad they're all young enough to be my sons. Even the officers are young."

We sat on stools around a small high table. We were surrounded by top guns, pilots of F-15s. The looks that passed between Remy and the fly boys registered an octane rating of Formula One racing fuel.

After we had a few drinks each and finished off a bowl of peanuts, Remy said, "These guys are too busy reliving the war and drowning the world's problems in booze to talk to us."

"They're not interested in us old bats," Angela cackled.

"Let's go." Remy stood up and we followed her out to her car.

We went to a Japanese restaurant in downtown Fort Walton Beach, where we sat on tatami mats on the floor around a lacquered table. We sipped the bartender's specialty, potent sake martinis with tiny pink umbrellas hooked over the rims of the glasses. We ordered sweet-sour soup, sukiyaki, cucumber salad, sashimi, and rice. The food was artfully arranged on the plates with a delicate balance of colors, shapes, and proportions.

"Use chopsticks. The food tastes better," I said, picking up a piece of cucumber with my lacquered sticks. Angela tried to pick up a strip of beef, but giggled and gave up. Remy didn't bother. She preferred to use a fork.

After her second sake martini, Angela quickly became stoned. She cackled so loudly that everyone in the restaurant stared at her. When Angela was sober, she was as stiff and silent as an inhibited Catholic-Italian nun. When she was drunk, she was as gleeful as a clam at high tide.

After dinner, we drank the remainder of the green tea in the pot and ordered Kahluas on the rocks.

Suddenly a shadow crossed Angela's face. She took a sip of her drink and looked at Remy. "Would you sleep with Vince if he wanted you to?"

Remy scowled. "Of course not. Why would you think that?

Besides, Vince wouldn't do that. You're drunk!"

Angela cackled belligerently. "Naw. Answer me. I wanna know." She twisted her wedding band around her finger.

Remy didn't say anything.

I wondered whether Remy had ever dated married men. I had noticed she was very friendly with the admiral she worked for and was becoming chummy with my boss, Jacob. Was this dalliance a delayed reaction to her years of faithfulness to Dan?

"Just because Dan died," Angela slurred, "you think other women's husbands are yours for the taking."

"I do not *take* anyone," Remy bristled. "Men come to me. After all, life is to be enjoyed. I want everyone around me to enjoy themselves, too."

"Never mind the heartache you cause." Angela's voice had reached a high pitch.

"I haven't broken any hearts."

Angela's jealousy was a form of flattery, but I thought she was obsessed by it. I paid the check and hurried the women out of the restaurant before the argument became louder and we were thrown out.

In our room, Angela plopped down on the sofabed.

Remy wasn't sleepy. "I'm going for a walk on the beach."

"It's almost midnight. It's dark out there," I said.

"I want to clear my head."

"You're not going alone. I'll go too." I wondered if we were sober enough to walk to the beach, but I wasn't going to let Remy go alone.

Angela dragged herself up from the couch. "Me too."

We changed to T-shirts, shorts, and sandals and made our way through the hotel's sandy grounds, onto the wooden walk that crossed over the dunes, and down to the water's edge.

The breeze off the Gulf was silkier than the river breeze in New Orleans. The sand was as fine as sugar under our feet, and the white dunes on the water's edge gleamed like snow in the moonlight. Lights from high-rise hotels and condominiums in Destin glittered along the shore that arced south of Fort Walton Beach.

Suddenly Angela staggered into the surf. Remy kicked off her sandals and waded into the cool water after her.

I knew Remy couldn't swim and I doubted Angela could, either. "Come back you two. Are you both off your rockers?"

Splashing in the surf, Angela lost her balance. She fell face down in the water. Remy bent down to grab Angela, but she fell too.

I plodded through the water. It seemed like an eternity before I reached the women. Remy rose onto her hands and knees and stood up, but she stumbled again as she tried to pull Angela to her feet.

When I reached them, I grabbed Angela's hand and pulled with all my strength. Her head rose to the surface of the water, which was only knee deep; then she stood up.

Remy, who had managed to stand up on her own, helped me lead a sputtering Angela towards the shore. On the beach, we landed Angela on the sand like a dead whale.

Angela gasped, "Thanks, Grace. You saved my life."

"No. Remy got to you first. You know she always thinks of her friends before herself."

Then Remy turned and headed out to sea again.

"Don't go any farther, Remy. Come back."

"Why?" Remy turned to wave at us. "I've got nothing to live for. Angela accuses me of stealing Vince."

"She didn't mean it. She's drunk. You have plenty to live for. Your friends love you. I love you. We need you." I waded after Remy as fast as I could. I reached Remy, put an arm around her, and turned her towards shore. Without much of a struggle, Remy let me lead her back to the beach, where we pulled Angela to her feet. We all walked slowly back to the hotel.

On the way, I thought perhaps my friends hadn't been in danger after all. Maybe Angela would have crawled to shore and Remy would have stumbled after her, but I knew that a tipsy woman, weighted down by wet clothes, could drown easily even in shallow water.

In the hotel room, Angela changed into her pajamas and fell asleep, snoring loudly, as her head hit the pillow on the sofabed.

Remy and I lay down on the two double beds. As I dropped off to sleep, I thought, what a night! I thanked God that every-thing had turned out all right.

On Sunday morning, Remy was making coffee in the room before Angela and I awoke. We checked out of the hotel, put our bags in the trunk of Remy's car, and went to brunch at a seafood restaurant on the beach road to Pensacola.

We began with martinis, then enjoyed a fried catfish lunch. On the way back to New Orleans, our conversation, as usual, got around to Bayou Beau.

"I was tired trying to please Beau. We had to break it off or get married. I guess we were getting too close to each other. Marriage might have been like a collision course."

"The sea of love is not Pacific," I commented.

"Besides, I got to know him too well. Some of his habits galled me. He belches, swears, picks his nose, and spits on the floor. His fart smells like shrimp, he eats so much of it."

"You were lucky to find all that out before you married him."

"And do you know what his idea of foreplay was?" She didn't wait for our answer. "He'd reach over in bed and say, '*Cherie*, are you sleeping?' Then, just before he puts it in, he raises on his elbows and bellows, 'Oh God, the saints are marching in'."

I groaned, "Some strange habits, all right."

Angela giggled and twisted her wedding band around her fin-ger.

After Remy dropped Angela off at her house, Remy turned to me.

"Life's hell without a lover."

"I don't miss men much," I said. "I haven't had a boyfriend in years. I can do without all that aggravation."

"It's good to get your ashes hauled once in a while."

"Ashes? I don't have a fireplace."

Remy laughed, "That's a southern expression meaning to have sex. Dan used to ask me if I wanted my ashes hauled."

"I guess some women feel sterile without a man," I said, thinking that Remy was like that. She had Pooh, but is a cat enough? Surely not for a loving, passionate, intelligent woman like Remy. She couldn't live without male attention.

"Don't you want to get married again?"

"Three times is enough," I laughed. "My marriages were battlefields and I'm staying out of the line of fire. Although, it would be nice to have a man around to take me dancing, out to dinner and theater, or cruise around the world."

"Yeah, but they always want something in return, right?"

"Amen."

When Remy parked in front of her apartment, she invited me in for a nightcap. Remy poured us a creme de menthe on the rocks. We sat on the livingroom sofa.

"Quite a weekend, eh?"

"Yes, it certainly was. Thanks for being there for me," said Remy.

I shrugged. "What are friends for?"

"I don't see Glenda and Hank often enough. They used to come to N'awlins frequently when Dan was alive, and we'd go over there some weekends."

"They think a lot of you."

"Yeah. Now, Hank's a man I could go for, if he weren't married, of course. I've always liked him."

The jangle of the phone startled us. "Would you mind answering that?" asked Remy.

"Sure, I'll get it."

"It's probably one of the heavy breathers or those jerks who hang up when I answer. I've been getting lots of those calls lately."

"Some dancehall romeo?"

Remy shrugged.

"Or maybe a jealous wife?"

Remy bristled, "I don't toy with married men."

When I picked up the receiver, I heard heavy breathing. I grabbed the whistle from my purse and blew it as hard as I could into the mouthpiece. Soon I heard a dial tone. "That should fix his or her eardrums."

"I hope so. Whoever it is often wakes me up in the middle of the night. Thanks."

We hugged and I left. As I hurried in the dark to my apartment, I wondered about Remy's phone calls. Could they be from an irate wife? For some reason, Remy's quick denial didn't ring true to me.

CHAPTER ELEVEN

During the winter after Remy broke up with Bayou Beau, her choice of men steadily worsened. She regarded sex as a wholesome indulgence, like dancing, martinis, and gourmet dinners.

Remy always dressed modestly at work, but after hours, she wanted to look sexy, to strike like greased lightning. Her marriage to Dan had kept her passions in check and made it safe for her to have close male, as well as female, friends. As a widow, she was free to follow her own inclinations. It was like opening a door that had been sealed for a long time.

With the intensity of an Olympian, she dated widowers looking for solace, divorced men still reeling from court, short or tall, bald or ponytailed, old, young, sweet, sad. Some of the men wanted to be her partner; others wanted to be her husband. She even met a few men who had enough ready cash to treat her in the manner to which Dan had accustomed her.

In singles bars, Remy juggled relationships with as many as four different men, each thinking he was the "only one." She put herself in danger. She went alone to bars, walked alone in rough neighborhoods, and invited men home before she really got to know them.

One morning I went into the coffee closet outside my office at the Facility and almost bumped into Remy and Jacob, who were giggling and snuggling together.

"Excuse me." I quickly poured a cup of coffee and hurried out of there.

Some days Remy asked me to come for lunch at her apartment so she could check on Pooh. On the way, we'd stop to buy a bucket of Kentucky Fried Chicken.

Gradually, Remy stopped asking me to lunch. I noticed Jacob was taking longer-than-usual lunch hours, sometimes two hours. One day in the parking garage, I saw Jacob and Remy getting into his car. I presumed they were driving to Remy's apartment for lunch.

One Monday morning, when Remy picked me up to go to work, she was yawning.

"Been up late?"

"I had a wonderful weekend. I flew to Washington, D.C. with the admiral."

"You did?" I was surprised. "I tried to call you Saturday."

"We flew up Saturday morning in his private jet. He's a pilot and has a P-39 for his personal use. We stayed at L'Enfante Hotel overlooking the Washington Monument and mall. It was wonderful. That evening we went out for a lobster dinner at Fisherman's Wharf. We flew back late last night."

I couldn't think of anything to say.

"We had separate hotel rooms, of course," Remy continued. "But we had drinks in my room, overlooking the Potomac River. It was so nice. He treats me like Dan did."

"Are you going to go out with him again?"

Remy smiled, "If he asks me."

"Won't his wife mind?"

"She thinks he goes to conferences in D.C., alone."

I was reminded of the British poet George Byron, who wrote something about adultery being more common where the climate's sultry.

"If I'd have known you were going to be away over the weekend, I'd have looked in on Pooh."

"Thanks, but it was a last-minute trip," said Remy. "Pooh was all right. She always has enough food and water."

"She gets lonely though."

One evening after a dance at the Desire Ballroom, Remy invited her current boyfriend, me, and a man I'd met several times, to her apartment for a nightcap. Remy made drinks for us, then she and her friend sprawled on the livingroom sofa. My friend and I sat in chairs across the room.

Remy's dress slipped off her bare shoulders and exposed part of her firm breasts. Her date was biting her lightly on the nape of the neck, throat, palms of her hands, and fingertips. Remy leaned back on one side of the sofa, and the man collapsed on top of her. Remy sighed softly and closed her eyes. They played kissyface and feelie-grabbie for a while.

I stood up and said to my date, "It's late. I think you ought to leave. I have to get up early tomorrow morning."

He agreed, reluctantly, and I walked him to the door in the hallway. After he left, I glanced into the livingroom where Remy's date was lifting up her blouse.

I said goodnight, but they didn't hear me.

On a Saturday in late July, Remy invited me for lunch in her apartment. When I stepped into the livingroom, I said, "Something smells wonderful in here. Like Mother's Restaurant. What are you cooking?"

"Red beans and rice."

"How come? This isn't Monday."

"I just felt like it."

This New Orleans' tradition stems from the days when women would put a pot of beans and rice to simmer on the back burner of their stoves while they did their laundry. The Facility's cafeteria even served red beans and rice each Monday for lunch.

"Most recipes call for dried kidney beans, which have to be soaked and cooked for several hours, before adding ham, ham hocks, or sausage. I made up a working-girl's version. It's very easy." Remy vigorously sautéed peppers, onions, garlic, and celery, as if she was sautéing the heart of her ex-lover rather than vegetables.

We carried bowls of red beans and rice to the dining table and sat down.

"This is delicious. No one would know it wasn't authentic," I said.

After lunch we spent the rest of the day at the World's Fair on the river's edge in downtown New Orleans. We sat for hours in the jazz tent, and Remy danced a few lively jitterbug numbers with some Texans.

While we had a snack before driving home, I decided it was a good time to break my news to Remy. I had been waiting for the right moment to tell her that I had accepted a promotion as technical editor with a Navy research lab in San Diego.

"I can't get a raise as long as Jacob is here, and he doesn't appear to be leaving, or retiring, any time soon. I hate to move, but it's the only way I can get ahead. I want to retire some day and, as you know, civil service retirement is based on your top three salaries. I'll miss writing news stories and features. I'll be editing reports written by research scientists, trying to put their big words into plain English so government officials in Washington can understand it and fund Navy projects."

"I understand, but I hate to see you go."

"I'll drive to California the last week in August. I have to report for work the Monday after Labor Day."

"Can I come with you?" Remy's face lit up. "I've got two weeks' leave saved up."

I smiled. "Do you mean it? I'd love that. We could take turns driving and we'd have fun along the way, I'm sure."

"We'll have a ball. Each night, we can stop at a motel and sit around the pool sipping martinis. Then get up early the next morning and be on the road again."

"Wonderful. It's all settled."

A month later, on my last Saturday evening in New Orleans, Remy and I went to Rex Rampart's bar in the Quarter. We parked in Dan's favorite garage and walked along Bourbon Street to the club. The air was filled with a purple neon haze and warmly redolent with the smell of beer and whiskey.

Bourbon Street, the hard-drinking and cool-jazz mecca of the country, is closed to vehicles at night. It becomes a pedestrian mall, congested with people, their faces happy and flushed.

The Quarter was gridlocked by nine p.m. and wilder than usual. Tulane was playing in the Dome on Sunday and the Saints were playing there on Monday. Rowdy fans were out by the thousands, parking everywhere, blocking streets, roaming in noisy mobs, drinking from plastic go-cups, and having a delightful time raising hell and enjoying life.

Hawkers tried to lure passers-by into their establishments, bouncers jettisoned unruly patrons from bars, and rockabilly, Dixieland, and the mellower sounds of jazz poured out of darkened barrooms and music halls. Spielers in straw boaters and candy-striped vests were plying their trade in front of the strip joints, Black kids danced and clattered their steel taps on the concrete, and Black steel bands jangled their tambourines and blared their horns.

Religious fanatics tried to buttonhole anyone to listen to their less hedonistic spiel, "Have you seen Jesus lately?"

Tourists from up North, Europe, and Japan rubbed elbows with Bourbon Street strippers, cross-dressers, hookers, mimes, singers, tapdancers, and homeless people pushing grocery carts with dogs leashed to the handles. The visitors carried hurricane glasses from Pat O'Brien's and plastic bags from T-shirt shops. One man wore a fabric hat made in the shape of a giant crawfish.

Our walk through the Quarter stretched to almost an hour. We stopped to listen to a man playing "Malaguena" on an accordian. The guy's dog took a dollar gently from my fingers and put it in his owner's hat on the ground.

The crowd gathered around another man standing on a small box. He wore a tux, white gloves, sneakers. His face was mime white and his hair was dressed in dreadlocks wrapped with gold braid that ended in a cluster of little wooden balls that jiggled when he moved. He stood with his arms raised and bent at the elbows, fingers spread in a flagrant display of bodily control. He shifted his arms to a new position and rotated his torso, becoming the Amazing Living Statue.

"I want to savor every sight and sound here. Who knows when I'll get back to New Orleans again."

Remy stopped to look in the window of a shop specializing in sex orgies. On display were black and white photos of a pile of naked bodies that resembled a drunken fraternity party. The shop next door sold erotic chocolate candy and cookies, such as edible erections, open zippers, and shaved-chocolate pubic hair.

In New Orleans the jazz and funk flow like water, and the musicians who play it tend to hang around the Big Easy like the humidity, refusing to leave for other parts of the country.

We peeked into Preservation Hall, where customers were packed three deep at the bar. The hall was about twice the size of a French Quarter hotel room and dim like the gloomy, candle-lit altar of a small country church. A half dozen wooden benches were lined up in front of the stage; everybody else, maybe seventy-five people, stood shoulder to shoulder in the darkness behind the benches. From a stage raised about eighteen inches from the floor, an eld-erly Black clarinetist, a white sax man, and a 300-pound white woman with flaming hair and sequined dress that sparkled like ice water were belting out the blues.

Down the street, the windows of Rex's Club announced, in neon script, "Cold Beer, Crawfish, Crabs, and Good Times." "Suck the Head!"

When we entered the club, Vince smiled and beckoned for us to sit at the end of the bar close to the band. We climbed up on stools.

I picked up a few pieces of munchies from the bowl that Vince set in front of us. "What is this? It looks like popcorn, but it has a spicy, fishy taste. It's good."

"That's Cajun popcorn," said Vince. "It's a spicy mixture of flakes of shrimp, crab, or crayfish fried in a cornmeal batter."

Vince set our drinks on the bar and winked at Remy. She was wearing an orange dress of soft, clinging fabric that hugged her body. Her cleavage was filled with gold chains of varied designs. Her trademark bangles encircled both wrists, and gold spheres almost the size of golf balls dangled from her ears.

The band was playing the "South Rampart Street Parade." Vince wiped the bar in front of us. "Did you know Steve Allen wrote the lyrics to this song?"

I nodded. "I wonder when he was here last?"

The club was crowded; the noise deafening. The bodies were as packed as a Mardi Gras crowd, everyone boogying in their own space. Couples jitterbugged like kids of the '40s, doing the bop, the dirty boogie, the twist, the shag. Some were dancing so close they appeared to be polishing each other's belt buckles.

Rex, a famed rhythm and blues musician, wore a sequined white coat, black pants, and black and white patent-leather shoes. He had a Rudolph Valentino parted-down-the-middle hair style. Rex gave the customers a good show for their money.

The crowd hushed when Bruno sat down at the piano. He wore a sequined purple coat and his black skin glowed with an electric sheen. He rocked from side to side as his ringed fingers caressed the keys. The notes rolled from one octave to the next, while saxophones and trumpets blared behind him. Then he sang, in a deep resonant voice, his killer rendition of "Old Man River."

Soon the band's singer came on stage. She wore a green, sequined dress that quivered as she crooned a twenties-style blues tune. Bruno harmonized with her low alto, sultry voice that warmed the atmosphere of the room like a sensuous embrace.

When the band played "When the Saints Go Marching In," the place went wild. The audience was a sea of dancing bodies, legs and arms akimbo, bobbing faces that whooped, screamed, and sang along to melodies they knew by heart.

Vince hovered around us, keeping our drinks topped off. He smiled at Remy and frequently patted her hand and arm. His smile seemed to beam into Remy, filling her with a warm glow that made her body behave like that of a woman about to make love. Remy seemed to long for Vince like a marathoner yearned for water halfway through a race. Vince gave every sign of the same thirst for Remy.

Something is going on there, I thought. I pretended not to notice the barefaced flirtation between my best friend and another friend's husband. There wasn't much chance of Vince doing anything out of line, since he was married, I hoped. Or was there?

During the band's break, Vince told Remy that Rex wanted to see her in his private office behind the bandstand. She went through the curtained door and disappeared for half an hour. Was Rex sweet on Remy too? If so, he was no different than a dozen other men.

"So do you think the Saints will win Monday night?"

"You can bet your life," Vince grinned.

"You have a lot of faith in that team. When was their last winning season?"

Before Vince could answer me, Remy returned, grinning slyly. Vince gave her another drink.

In the wee hours just before the bar closed, the band played W.C. Handy's "St. Louis Blues." "I hate to see the evenin' sun go down... Cause my baby done gone and left this town. Feelin' tomorrer jes' like I feel today... I'll pack my trunk an' make my getaway."

"Guess that's our cue to pack our bags, too," I said to Remy.

"Not 'til you have a nightcap," said Bruno, leading us to a table. "Hey, Vince, fix us some drinks, will you?"

"Sure," Vince grinned. "Give me a few minutes."

Bruno dropped a quarter into the juke box. Pete Fountain's "New Orleans, Tennessee" came through the speakers.

"Oh, I like that song," said Remy as the smooth, dreamy piece surrounded us. "It's like dancing close to someone you love."

The words were the same throughout the song... "I'm going back to New Orleans, Tennessee, and I ain't gonna leave...and I ain't gonna leave."

After Vince finished clearing the bar and tables, he sat down with us. While Bruno and I talked about musicians' night life, Vince and Remy huddled together.

Remy whispered, "You're good for me."

"We were meant to be together. I know it and you know it. You won't admit it. We're not kids anymore. It's later than you think."

Remy blushed. She made a furtive motion with her right hand, as if she were withdrawing it unobtrusively from Vince's hand that she had been holding under the table. Remy tried to unfold her cocktail napkin, but her fingers shook badly. Arthritis or guilt?

Remy and I stood up to leave. Vince hugged Remy as though she were never coming back.

"Tell Angela goodbye for me, will you, Vince?"

"Sure, Grace. We'll miss you."

"See ya soon," Vince said to Remy.

Remy and I walked to the parking garage in the shank of the night. Every other playground in the country either winds down or closes at 2 a.m., but not Bourbon Street. A saxophonist played a soulful song from his spot on the sidewalk. Someone named Desiree was being called to bed. Tourists, conventioneers, street people, night people, gamblers, prostitutes, hustlers, cops, couples, musicians, sidewalk entertainers, and hot dog salesmen strolled about. They seemed to be reluctant to return to their hotel rooms or homes.

On the drive home, I wondered what was down the road for myself. Was I doing the right thing by leaving my friends, music, and a city I loved? As for Remy, I couldn't imagine what her future might hold, but I was concerned about her.

Early the next morning, after only a few hours' sleep, Remy and I left New Orleans. The back of my Ford Mustang was stuffed with clothes and items I'd need in San Diego until my household goods arrived.

That first day we drove 700 miles and arrived in San Antonio in early evening. We checked into the historic Hotel Minter, across the alley from the Alamo. The hotel was full and we couldn't get adjoining rooms, so we had to take a double room.

When Remy opened her suitcase, I saw red silky bikini panties, lacy teddies, and push-up bras that must have come straight
from Victoria's Secret. In our annual exchange of birthday and
Christmas gifts, Remy usually received provocative, and expensive, pieces of lingerie from one of us. At night, especially when
traveling, Remy preferred to wear modest opaque nightshirts that
reached to her knees.

Remy and I strolled along the River Walk in the heart of San
Antonio until we chose an inviting-looking restaurant to have dinner on the terrace beside the flowing water. In the foyer of the
restaurant, I picked up a brochure about the history of the River
Walk.

While we enjoyed a combination Mexican dinner, I read that
the River Walk opened in 1941, with expectations of becoming an
American Venice. But by 1960 that dream had faded and the area
was not a choice place to be after dark. The walk's glory days arrived after it was refurbished for the 1968 HemisFair. Today, the
river banks are lined with hotels, inns, restaurants, and an unceas-
ing flow of visitors.

After dinner, Remy and I ambled farther along the river on the
wide sidewalk, beneath cottonwood trees rustling in the breeze.
Torch-lit barges gliding down the river were crammed with passengers smiling and tapping their feet to the rhythm of the mariachi
bands on board. We crossed one of the arched stone bridges over
the river and returned to our hotel.

Early the next morning, Remy and I ate breakfast in a Mexican café in old town. On the walk back to the hotel, we toured the
Spanish Governor's Palace and then stopped at the Alamo. Inside,
a plaque hanging on the wall mentioned that the Alamo had been
an abandoned mission house.

"I'm glad we stopped here," Remy said. "Dan wanted to come
to San Antonio, especially to visit the Alamo."

"What was his interest in this place?"

"Some of his ancestors fought here during the Texas revolution. He'd have loved to see this place," said Remy. "He should
have been a historian, I guess, instead of an Air Force officer...."

"Well, he was in a way. He was helping to restore the old New Orleans mint."

"Yeah. He was always a history buff."

"Isn't this the Jim Bowie who invented the Bowie knife?" I pointed to a historical plaque that honored Bowie, a hero of the Texas revolution who died at the Alamo. "Beau said the Bowie knife was named for him. Speaking of Beau, I wonder how he's doing?"

Remy shrugged, "Maybe he's found another girlfriend."

By noon, Remy and I were on the road heading west. August had dug in its heels. We quickly changed from jeans to shorts and sleeveless shirts. In the back of the car, we kept a cooler filled with ice, fruit juice, oranges, apples, crackers, cheese, and cold cuts. We stopped on the road at rest areas to eat picnic lunches.

At Fort Stockton, an overland stage stop, we took time to visit the Annie Riggs Hotel Museum. Pulling into Sonora, Texas, late afternoon, we lolled around the pool at the Devil's River Motel. During dinner at the adjacent Sutton County Steakhouse, the eyes of all the cowboy customers were on Remy. Of course, she flirted with them. The way she tilted her head when she looked at a man made him think he was the only male in the universe. Her sparkling eyes and husky, intimate voice hooked every man in sight.

The next afternoon, we drove into El Paso and stayed in adjoining rooms at the Howard Johnson Motel, perched on a hill overlooking the city.

In the morning, when a guide/driver picked us up for a tour of Juarez, Mexico, Remy immediately turned on her charms. She linked arms with him as we toured the Chamizol National Monument, a glass factory, the city market, an old mission, the Monument Bull Ring, country club residential area, race track, industrial park, and the Pronof Center.

Remy was disappointed when our guide didn't join us for lunch in a Mexican restaurant. He excused himself and said he'd be back in an hour to continue the tour. During the afternoon, we rode through downtown El Paso, skirting the Rio Grande, through the campus of the University of Texas and its Sun Bowl, caught a glimpse of Mt. Franklin, passed by Fort Bliss, and visited the Tigua Indian Reservation.

Remy and I left early the next morning. By late afternoon, we were in Tombstone, Arizona, where we checked into the Best Western Motel. Both of our rooms featured a cornflower blue-painted swinging door between the bedroom and bath.

We walked around town, watched Wyatt Earp's shoot-out enactment, and visited the Bird Cage Theater Museum. We ate a surprisingly tasty lobster dinner at Big Nose Kate's saloon. Afterwards, we had drinks in a bar where we danced with men employed at the communications stations located in the nearby hills.

We returned to the motel very late. Early the next morning, we headed west on I-10.

The next night we stayed in a hotel in Yuma, Arizona. While we were sipping martinis beside the pool, the sky fell out. Rain and wind attacked the town and desert with hurricane force. The weather was too nasty to venture out to find a restaurant, so we ate bowls of Tex-Mex chile in the hotel's diningroom.

As we went to our separate rooms, Remy said, "I think I'll call mother tonight. She looks forward to my weekly calls."

Every time I knocked on Remy's door, she was on the phone. Remy must be racking up a huge bill on her phone credit card, I thought. Besides her mother, who else was Remy calling? Surely not Beau. Was it Vince? I didn't ask and I never found out.

When we left the next morning, the Yuma River had overflowed, flooding the streets of the city. After driving 2,184 miles, we arrived in San Diego and rented rooms at a motel in Point Loma. Sunday morning after breakfast, we drove past the Navy laboratory where I was to start work Monday, and to the Cabrillo Monument at the end of Point Loma, where San Diego Bay meets the Pacific Ocean.

Remy packed her suitcase early Monday morning. She was ready when her son-in-law arrived to drive her back to Los Angeles to spend a few days with the family.

I hugged Remy. "I'll miss you so much. You've been a wonderful friend, and you're a great traveling companion. I don't know what I'll do without you."

"I'll miss you too, Grace. We'll keep in touch."

I waved as Remy and her son-in-law drove off.

CHAPTER TWELVE

A year later Remy retired at age 62. She thought she could live up to her accustomed style on her civil service annuity, plus Dan's military pension. She decided to retire when the arthritis in her shoulder and hands pained so much she couldn't type or take shorthand as well as she used to. She felt she was not doing a good job, although her admiral boss denied that.

Remy said her doctor had prescribed medicine to ease her arthritis pain, but she didn't want to take it. Maybe she thought martinis and sex would do the trick.

The week after Remy retired, I received a letter from Ellen. As usual, her letter was filled with details.

"Dear Grace,

The Facility invited Alex and me to Remy's retirement luncheon at the Court of Two Sisters on Royal Street. It was lovely. Everyone from work was there, even the admirals. Angela and Vince came into town, too.

Did you know that the restaurant is located on the site of a 19th century notions shop? It was owned by two Creole sisters who outfitted many of the city's finest women with Parisian gowns, lace, and perfumes.

Anyway, we helped ourselves from sixty dishes in the Jazz Brunch Buffet, set up in the gaslit courtyard. Then we took our plates into the private Grand Marquis Room. The food was delicious. Employees had taken up a collection and gave Remy a four-figure check. She was very surprised.

Now that Remy's retired, she and Angela are closer than ever. They see each other almost every day to go shopping or to Weight Watcher's meetings. That's a laugh. I hear that after the meetings, they go to a bar for a few drinks. They also joined a health spa on the lake front and go twice a week to exercise and soak in the hot tub.

Well, that's all for now. Keep in touch.

Fondly, Ellen."

Remy called me two weeks later.

"How do you like retirement?" I asked her.

"I miss the people at work, but my arthritis got so bad I couldn't be the secretary I once was. My thumbs and shoulders hurt most of the time. I ignore the pain."

"What do you do with your days now?"

"I still go with Angela and Vince to Sunday brunch. Angela and I joined a senior lunch club in East New Orleans. Guess who was elected secretary-treasurer?"

I laughed, "You, of course. Who else but the best secretary the Facility ever had?"

"I even bought a typewriter to write minutes and letters for the club."

"Have you met any interesting men at the dances?"

Remy snorted, "No. I only go occasionally. Did I tell you that my mother died?"

"No. I'm so sorry."

"She died peacefully in her sleep. She was eighty-seven. She led a full life, and I think she enjoyed her last years in the nursing home. I went to New York for the funeral. Jacquie and her dad were there, too. Well, guess that's all the news."

"Take care."

Later that year, Remy called me to say she was coming to San Diego to scout for an apartment. She couldn't decide whether she could afford to live in California, but thought she should give it a whirl. Besides, she'd like to be closer to Jacquie so she could see her granddaughters grow up.

In San Diego, Remy stayed with me in my Mission Hills apartment. She scoured the want-ads daily, but couldn't find a price or location to suit her. Then she went to Los Angeles, where she spent a week at her daughter's and looked at several apartments.

When Remy returned to New Orleans, she called me.

"Hi. I've decided I can't afford to move to California. Besides, I'd miss New Orleans, and my friends. The food, the music. You know the song, 'Do you know what it means to miss New Orleans?' Well, I found out."

"Yea. I miss it, too. But I was looking forward to having you nearby. I don't think you looked hard enough. I'll bet you could find a place outside of L.A. that you could afford. Well, it's up to you. What else did you do while you were there?"

"I went to Lake Arrowhead."

"That's a pretty place. What did you do there?"

Remy hesitated. "I stayed at Vince's cousins' cabin. Vince was there for a few days. We had a wonderful time."

"Was the whole family there, too?"

"No, we were alone. He's so sweet and huggable, like a Teddy Bear."

"What does Angela think about that?"

"I don't think she knows."

"Well, take care."

When I hung up, I wondered about Remy and Vince. Were they seeing each other? I was suspicious, but I was living too far away to do anything about it. But then what could I have done? They're both adults, seniors at that.

A few months later, Remy sent me a picture of her new look. She had her red hair dyed blonde. On the back, she wrote: "Yes, blondes do have more fun."

I thought Remy looked better as a redhead, but I didn't dare tell her. To each her own, I thought. As a blonde, Remy needed a little more makeup but not much, just a dab of powder and brighter rouge and lipstick.

I sensed that going blonde was Remy's turning point. She

wanted to show the world that she'd changed. She was probably wearing more revealing V-neck dresses, shorter skirts, see-through blouses. I was sure she was still in pain, but she was taking her life into her own hands.

Several months later, my boss in San Diego assigned me temporary duty to work on a special project at the Pensacola Naval Air Station, Florida. I jumped at the chance.

The transportation officer booked me on a Navy plane to Pensacola. The aircraft was full, mostly with airmen and officers. When I took my seat, I didn't notice the Navy captain sitting beside me, but soon I felt him looking at me. He was reading a magazine, but from time to time his eyes slipped over the top of the page and glanced quickly at my legs. I could feel his eyes on me, and I buttoned one of the top two buttons of my shirt.

The captain turned to me and smiled, "Would you like to come with me to the lav?"

"I beg your pardon?" The jerk was trying to pick me up.

"Are you a member of the Mile High Club?"

"What?" I was startled.

"The Mile High Club." He winked and opened his jacket to reveal a Mile High Club T-shirt.

I stared at the shirt on which was painted an airplane with winking eyes and, flapping in the breeze out of a window, were a bra, panty hose, and boxer shorts.

"Oh, I've heard of the club." I remembered it was about sex at a mile high, or more. "I saw it in action during a flight between New York and Rio de Janeiro. It would be pretty daring to do that on a military aircraft. I'm sure it's frowned upon."

He nudged my arm. "Come with me to the lav. No pun intended. I'll bet you've already earned your wings."

I groaned. "No thanks." I picked up a paperback novel from my carry-on bag and didn't look up for the rest of the flight.

The Navy Air Force project manager met me at Pensacola Naval Air Station and drove me to the bachelor officers' quarters. I left

my suitcase in my room and went with him to his office. I finished
the project in four days.

I took leave on Friday and hopped a ride with an airman to
Remy's apartment in New Orleans. That evening Remy and I went
to the Santorinis' house for cocktails. We all hugged each other.
Remy embraced Vince with both arms, fiercely, and in full view of
Angela. He laughed and held Remy's head close to his. Over her
head, he grinned at his wife.

"Drinks, Vince." Angela's smile was thin.

Immediately, Vince let go of Remy and made us vodkas on the
rocks. He handed the drinks to us and we settled in the livingroom
to talk.

"It's great that you could come to Pensacola on TDY," said
Vince. "We've missed you."

"Thanks. I've missed you all, too. I was lucky to be assigned
there. My Navy flight was pleasant except for my seatmate, a Navy
captain. He tried to pick me up."

"Well, why not? You can't blame a guy for trying, eh?" Vince
winked at me.

"He wanted to initiate me into the Mile High Club in a military plane. Can you believe that?"

Remy laughed, "Oh, let me tell you about that."

"I can hardly wait."

"I joined the Mile High Club on a first-class flight from Washington, D.C., to New Orleans. One weekend when I flew to Washington with the admiral in his military plane, he had to stay in the
capital for a meeting, so he sent me back to New Orleans first-class
on a commercial flight. My seatmate on the jet was a dashing
Latin diplomat who was returning home to Colombia. He told me
he was going to the lav and asked if I wanted to join him. I was
startled at first. Then I thought, why not? Live it up. I was horny
after spending a day with the admiral. So the Latino and I went
into the tiny lavatory and had a quickie. Talk about cramped! Anyway, when we came out, a flight attendant congratulated me and
pinned a set of wings on my lapel."

Angela chortled.

"You're wicked," I teased her. "I understand that the Mile High Club sells caps, T-shirts, caps, and gifts."

"Some airlines advertise that passengers can fly on custom-outfitted aircraft for their aerial pleasures. They operate out of New York, Ohio, Colorado, and, of course, California," said Remy.

"Things haven't changed much since you left," said Angela, twirling the cocktail glass around in her hand. "Vince still plays poker every Sunday evening with members of Rex's band, or so he tells me. I keep asking Remy to come over to keep me company on Sunday evenings, but she is always busy."

Remy smiled but didn't say anything.

"Do you doubt me?" asked Vince.

"I'm really getting suspicious." Angela's voice had a terrible edge to it like she was holding back a flood of angry words. "One of the wives told me that the poker games were getting less frequent."

"Who told you that? She's wrong."

"Surely you're not having another affair at your age, 73. When you come home late at night you don't even kiss me goodnight or check to see if I'm asleep."

"What do you mean?" Vince stood up. "I'm the perfect husband these days." He glanced across the room at Remy moments longer than he should have, then looked away.

Angela chortled, "You'd better not be cheating on me. If I find out you are, I'll leave you."

"You wouldn't leave me," Vince laughed.

"Why not? Because you're so adorable?"

"Because I'll get my gun and shoot you," Vince said with a poker face.

"Not if I shoot you first." She shook her finger at him.

Angela's casual talk about killing Vince made my skin crawl. I didn't know whether she was trying to intimidate Vince or Remy or me. She could have been testing us by talking about something so gruesome in a light, humorous way. We didn't take her seriously.

Vince laughed and kissed Angela on the cheek. "I've got to get to work. You ladies have fun tonight."

After Vince let, Remy said, "I don't think Vince is running around. He loves you too much. After all, you've been married 40 years, right?"

"Still, I can't help wondering. You know that he's had affairs in the past...." Angela's voice sounded like she had a Jew's harp stuck in her throat.

"I wasn't sure."

"I remember one showgirl he was wild about. Trixie Lee. What a floozy. That lasted a year. When I found out, he quit seeing her. Italians value family life. He'd never leave me. If I ever do find out he's fooling around, I'll put a hex on her."

"Would you really use voodoo?" I was afraid Angela was going to do something rash.

"You betcha. Hoodoo is alive and well in New Orleans," Angela grinned, her lips stretched tightly as a rubber band. Tucking her gold cross under her blouse, she held up a silver charm suspended from a chain around her neck. The charm was a hollow filigree sphere, filled with herbs. "If I wear this close to my body, I can control his thoughts. I'll haunt him day and night, driving him nuts. He won't be able to run after anyone else."

I shivered as I listened to her bone-chilling speech. The drama of infidelity rarely unfolds privately; like a slow hiss in a punctured tire, the news leaks out. Some people blame it on the wife. Angela was usually drunk when Vince came home. I knew that in this day and age, it was fashionable to minimize, even romanticize, adultery. The attitude was to follow your heart and damn the consequences. In truth, betrayal is a horrible, destructive beast, damaging everything in its path: those who betray and those betrayed.

Remy drove Angela and me to a new French restaurant in East New Orleans, where we enjoyed a delicious repast of salad, rack of baby lamb, rice with red pepper, and artichoke bottoms with gruyere and Parmesan in mornay sauce.

Angela suddenly turned to Remy. "Did you see Vince at his cousins' cabin at Lake Arrowhead last summer?"

Remy chewed an artichoke leaf for what seemed like an eon. "Yes. I went up there one day."

"Was anyone else there? A woman. His girlfriend?"

"No. He was alone." She patted her lips with her linen napkin.

"Hmmph." Angela turned up the edges of her cucumber as though she expected something alive to be buried underneath.

I didn't like the way the conversation was going. The talk was heading toward disaster. "What are we going to do tomorrow, Remy?"

"Well, I thought we could go to the Quarter in the morning, then Ellen told me to bring you out for dinner."

"Sounds great to me."

Monday morning, Remy drove me back to Pensacola. On the Navy flight to San Diego, I thought about Remy. She acted like she didn't have a care in the world. How long would her euphoria last?

CHAPTER THIRTEEN

"You'll never guess what happened," Remy called me in San Diego one evening.

"No, I can't. Tell me."

"Last night I ran into Beau at the Do Drop Inn. We talked, danced a little, and went back to my apartment. He's been spying on me, I think, because he asked me who I had been dating. He tried to call me Sunday evenings to chat, but I didn't answer the phone.

"Beau said he loved me and still wanted to marry me. I couldn't believe it. He hasn't found anyone else. He asked me to take back his engagement ring. I was surprised that he hadn't hocked it. Anyway, I agreed. Who else do I have? I need a man around. You know how hard it is to find a good man these days. Beau may not be perfect, but he'll do."

"Well, if he makes you happy. What about his ex-wife and 'Tit Gard? And what about all his habits that disgust you?"

"Fortunately, his ex-wife remarried and is very happy. She seldom calls him. And 'Tit Gard is attending junior college and lives on campus. As for Beau's strange habits, I guess I'll get used to them eventually."

"Do you love him?"

"You know, Beau is a gentleman and he respects me. We like each other's company. Oh sure, we have our differences, but we both have love to give."

"When's the wedding?"

"I'll let you know. You must be here."

"I wouldn't miss it."

"First, I have to break off with someone I've been seeing," Remy said.

"Anyone I know?"

Remy was silent.

"Well, keep in touch, Remy. I miss you."

"Miss you too. 'Bye."

I replaced the receiver in its cradle. Has Remy been seeing Vince? I was pretty sure she had. Was Remy willing to take second best? Had she really recovered from Dan's death?

Three days later, Ellen wrote to me.

"Dear Grace,

Remy tells me Bayou Beau still wants to marry her. He asked her not to see whoever she was dating anymore. I wondered who she had been seeing? Do you know?"

Anyway, Remy told Beau she would accept his ring after she broke up with her current male companion. I can't believe she could be happy with Beau, but perhaps she thinks he's her last chance. All these years I've overlooked Alex's rough edges, but he's made a good living and he's always been faithful to me. Maybe that's how Remy feels about Beau. Well, I'll let you know what happens.

Fondly, Ellen.

P.S. Here's my Shrimp Creole recipe you asked for. It's easy to make."

I wish I could have been a fly on the wall that Sunday evening when Remy planned to break off things with whomever she was seeing. I was pretty sure it was Vince. This is what I imagined happened.

Vince must have rushed into Remy's apartment, hugged her, and turned on his charming smile that she found so irresistible. His smile started in his eyes and traveled to his sensuous mouth; it melted her heart.

Remy probably told Vince they couldn't go on like they were.

What they were doing was wrong. What if Angela found out? She was already suspicious.

Vince no doubt denied that Angela knew anything about them. She still thinks I'm out with Rex and the boys, he'd say.

Then Remy burst out with the story that she had agreed to marry Beau. After all, she reasoned, Beau wasn't married, and they didn't have to sneak around like she and Vince did.

Of course, Vince pleaded with Remy not to stop seeing him. He loved her. They'd known each other for twenty years. His evenings with Remy were all the pleasure he had, he'd plead. After many tears and hugs, they went into the bedroom to make love for the last time.

CHAPTER FOURTEEN

Nothing seemed out of the ordinary when I woke up that morning in November. Routinely, I showered, dressed, and made breakfast.

From my Point Loma office, I stared out the window at the Pacific Ocean. I was restless. Was something about to happen? I couldn't imagine what.

The telephone's jangle snapped me back to reality.

"Grace? Are you sitting down? I have very bad news."

"What is it, Ellen?"

Silence.

"Tell me, Ellen."

"Remy's dead."

I almost dropped the phone. "What?"

"She was shot last night."

"You mean one of those dancehall Romeos went berserk and killed her?"

"No. Worse."

"What could be worse?"

"Angela shot her."

"What?"

"Remy never regained consciousness. She died at Humana Hospital, all alone. She was only 63."

"Oh my God." I felt like crying, vomiting, and screaming all at once.

"Evidently Vince and Remy were having an affair. Why didn't we realize that?"

"Maybe we did know deep down inside us. We didn't want to believe it was true," I said. "Several times I thought something was going on between them, but I was afraid to say anything. If only we could have done something, she'd be alive today."

"Guess we were too hard on Beau, always telling Remy he wasn't good enough for her."

"Yes, maybe. Twenty-twenty hindsight doesn't help us now. It's too late for regrets, Ellen. "

"Oooh, I'm afraid so. I'm just thankful that Remy's mother died before this happened. This would have killed her for certain."

"Have you been to Remy's apartment?"

"Yes. Jacquie and her husband flew in from California and rented a car. Alex and I met them at the apartment. The bed had been stripped, and there was a chalk outline where Remy fell beside the bed. Pooh was hiding under the bed. She hadn't had water or food in two days."

I choked up.

"Are you still there, Grace?" Ellen filled in the silence. "I'll save a copy of the *Times Picayune* article for you. It was short. It said that Angela shot Remy during an argument. Angela was arrested and charged with second-degree murder. Grace?"

"Yes. I'm in shock."

"We all are. Do you think you'll be able to come to the funeral? It's the day after tomorrow. Alex and I want you to stay with us."

"I don't know. I'm a basket case right now. I'll let you know."

By afternoon, the realization of Remy's death struck me with the force of a bullet. I pulled myself together enough to call my travel agent.

Later at home, I brooded over a dry martini or two. The drinks reminded me of the many martinis Remy and I had drank together. Then I packed a suitcase.

In the morning, I caught a flight from San Diego to New

Orleans. When the aircraft reached cruising altitude, I ordered a double Bloody Mary. While I sipped it slowly, I thought about Remy. I tried to imagine the scene in Remy's apartment when Angela caught Vince and Remy together. Did Angela mean to shoot Vince? Or Remy? Her death was even more tragic because it came at the hands of her best friend.

The plane dipped a wing toward Lake Pontchartrain and banked for its final descent. Through the window, I saw the gray-blue waters of the lake, touched with whitecaps, and the white dots of sailboats farther off. As the plane lowered toward Moissant Field, I made out the green oval of the infield at Jefferson Downs, the streets of Kenner, and cars moving along the Eastern Expressway. With a flap-down shriek of brakes, the plane landed on the grease-burned tarmac of New Orleans International Airport.

When I walked through the automatic doors of the terminal, Ellen and Alex O'Reilly were waiting for me at the curb. Alex put my suitcase in the trunk of his car, and we drove away from the logjam of buses, taxis, and courtesy vans and onto the freeway.

CHAPTER FIFTEEN

At their house, Ellen put the finishing touches on a pot-roast dinner. Their tiger cat, Patty, named because she was born on St. Patrick's Day, watched Ellen from the window sill above the kitchen sink. When Ellen opened the oven door to baste the roast with butter, the aroma from the beef juices steamed out of the oven like incense. Patty, her whiskers twitching, moved closer to the stove.

"Dinner will be ready as soon as I make the Caesar salad," Ellen said. A few minutes later, she gave the salad a final toss and spooned it onto three plates. Then she arranged slices of meat on a platter and surrounded it with tender carrots and potatoes.

As we sat down at the table, Alex licked his lips. "This is what I call comfort food. Meat and potatoes. Nothing like it."

We ate dinner silently. Afterwards, Ellen served coffee and apple pie.

The basic journalist's questions spun around in my mind: Who? What? When? Where? Why? How? I shifted restlessly in my chair. "We've avoided talking about Remy long enough. Tell me what happened."

Ellen reached out to the sideboard and picked up three newspaper clippings. "Read these." She handed me the articles.

"A woman died after being shot during an argument with another woman at an eastern New Orleans apartment Sunday night, police said.

The woman, 63, whose name was withheld pending notification of relatives, died at Humana Hospital shortly after the 8:40 p.m. shooting, New Orleans Police Department spokesman said.

The other woman, Angela Santorini, 69, also of eastern New Orleans, remained on the scene after the shooting and was arrested on murder charges.

A .22-caliber pistol was used in the shooting which occurred in the woman's bedroom in her Kenilworth apartment.

Santorini's husband, Vince, who was also in the apartment, called the police."

The second article didn't add much to the first.

"A woman shot to death Sunday night in her eastern New Orleans apartment was identified as Remy Rawley, 63.

Police booked Angela Santorini, 69, with second-degree murder. Santorini was released from the Orleans Community Correctional Center on a property bond Monday."

An item in the obituary column stated: "Relatives and friends of the family, also Senior Citizens Shepherd Center, are invited to attend the funeral of Remy Rawley at the Gentilly Home of Tharp-Sontheimer-Laudumiey, 5001 Chef Menteur Hwy, Thursday, Sept. 24, at 9 o'clock a.m. Following religious services in the parlor, interment will be in Biloxi National Cemetery."

When I'd written obituaries in the course of almost half a century as a newspaper reporter and editor, I tried to distance myself from the ever-present sorrow of obits. I couldn't do that now.

"These are just the facts," I said, putting the clippings back on the sideboard. The stories spelled an end to my friend's life. "They forgot to mention that Remy was a retired employee of the Navy Facility and the beloved wife of the late Daniel Rawley, mother of Jacquie Sanchez of California. She is also survived by two grandchildren."

"I don't think we'll ever know what really happened. Vince isn't talking," said Ellen.

"Why didn't we realize Remy and Vince were having an affair?"

Ellen shook her head.

"I gave Vince more credit than that," said Alex, relighting his cigar. "I thought he'd have enough sense not to fool around with his wife's best friend."

"I guess you never really know your friends, even those close to you." I took a bite of pie.

"Do you think Angela meant to kill Vince *and* Remy?" Ellen asked.

"If it had been me, I'd have killed Vince first," I said.

Alex guffawed, "Naw. Angela still wanted Vince."

"Angela was probably loaded with vodka before she called a taxi and went to Remy's apartment," said Ellen.

"I know Vince kept a loaded .22 in the nightstand beside their bed," said Alex. "He bought it after their house had been broken into several times and a window of his Oldsmobile had been smashed. That neighborhood isn't like the old days, when everyone knew each other."

"Angela had to get a taxi. You know she had her driver's license revoked years ago for drunk driving. She almost killed a boy who ran across the street in front of her one day. She was too drunk to stop. After that, Vince sold her car and wouldn't let her drive," said Ellen.

"Angela must have arrived at the apartment in a killing rage, all pumped up," I said.

"She shot Remy in the abdomen. They were both a bloody mess, according to the police," Alex said.

"Oooh. And Pooh was on the bed watching it all."

"Where was Vince?"

"When Remy and he heard the knock at the front door, they must have known who was there, so Vince hid in the bathroom," said Alex.

"Vince must have come out of the bathroom when he heard the shot. He called 911. Detectives and paramedics arrived within minutes and took Remy to Humana Hospital. It was too late. She died all alone," said Ellen.

"Well, detectives had an open and shut case," said Alex. "Vince told them what happened and Angela didn't try to run away or deny it."

"A smoking gun case, eh?"

"What do you mean?"

"That's what detectives call it when the guilty party is still at the scene when they arrive," I explained.

Later, in the O'Reilly's spare bedroom, I tossed and turned. I tried to recreate the night of Remy's murder. My guess was it must have happened somewhat like this.

That Sunday evening, Angela realized that Remy and Vince were seeing each other. After Vince left the house, presumably to play poker with the band boys, she drank several vodka tonics. She guessed their affair had started in the Lake Arrowhead cabin. She was blinded by rage. Remy was a friend of the family, her best friend. Angela might have gone into her altar room, the closet she had transformed after her oldest daughter married and moved away. Perhaps she thought about sticking pins in a doll. Maybe that seemed too tame for her. Or too slow.

So around eight o'clock, Angela decided to find out for herself. She called a taxi and went to Remy's apartment. She pounded on Remy's door and Remy, wearing a pink Minnie Mouse nightshirt, opened it.

"Angela! What do you want?" She and Vince were convinced that Angela didn't know about them and suspected nothing.

Angela shoved the door wide open and rushed past Remy into the livingroom. "Where is he?"

"Who?"

Angela cackled, "*Merde.* Don't lie to me. I know Vince is here. How long has this been going on?"

"I don't know what you're talking about. He's not here."

Angela howled like an angry hyena seeking its prey. She really got mad then and started hitting Remy, backing her into the bedroom. They tangled violently, pulling hair, scratching each other's face. Angela jabbed Remy's mouth and split her lip. Blood dribbled down her chin. Then they fell to the floor and began kicking each other.

As Angela shoved Remy against the bed, she yanked the .22 pistol out of her purse. She pointed the gun at Remy.

"Don't shoot. Please don't shoot," Remy pleaded.

Suddenly the bathroom door opened and Vince stepped out.

Angela pointed the gun at him. "You coward! Don't you have the guts to face me? Maybe I'll shoot you both."

Vince probably put his arm around Remy's shoulders. "Don't shoot. It's not her fault."

Angela clutched the gun with both hands.

Before Angela pulled the trigger, Remy stepped in front of Vince. She wanted to protect Vince. That was her way.

The bullet struck below Remy's waist. The lead tore through her abdomen and exploded inside. Blood began to ooze around the wound. She clutched her stomach. Her arm knocked the Mickey Mouse telephone off the nightstand as she fell to the floor.

"My God, Angela, what have you done?" Vince dropped to his knees and held Remy's lifeless head to his chest, then picked up the receiver and called 911.

Pooh leaped off the bed and licked Remy's limp, bloody hand.

After tossing and turning all night, I got up the next morning feeling like death warmed over. After I dressed, the aromas of scrambled eggs, sizzling bacon, and freshly baked biscuits led me into the dining room, where Alex and Ellen were seated at the kitchen table.

"Good morning. Did you sleep all right?" Ellen poured me a cup of coffee.

"No. I kept picturing the murder scene."

"Have some breakfast. It'll be a long day."

I bit into a biscuit, light as a feather and crunched on a piece of bacon. "I miss your cooking, Ellen."

"Oooh."

Later in the morning, Remy's memorial service was held at the same funeral parlor on Chef Menteur Highway in Gentilly, where Dan's services had been held.

There were half a dozen floral arrangements, including Ellen's and mine in the room. Only a few mourners attended the service.

It was a pitiful remembrance for such a generous, passionate woman who loved life.

Jacquie, her husband, and her father were there. Also, Alex, Ellen, three women from the senior club, and myself. I wondered why Bruno and Rex Rampart hadn't come to pay their last respects to a woman they both admired.

Vince wasn't there. I didn't know whether I was glad that he had the good grace, or cowardice, to stay away, or whether I wanted to confront him, to lash out at him for letting Remy protect him from Angela's rage.

It's a good thing Vince didn't come because Bayou Beau dashed into the chapel at the last minute. He wore dark glasses. He strode to my side as if he were going to a fight. He would have most likely knocked Vince's face off if he'd seen him.

Beau hugged me. "*Mon Dieu.* Remy and I were going to be married as soon as possible. You know I loved her very much."

I nodded, "You'll never know how much I wished you two had gotten married. She was my best friend. I'll miss her."

"Mine too. *C'est vrai.* If only we hadn't broken up." Beau was pale, completely unmanned. "Last Saturday, Remy, and everyone, came to my camp for a picnic. We had a ball. It was like old times between Remy and me. I didn't know I cared so much for her."

"Too late, Beau." I turned and walked to the front of the room to see Remy for the last time.

The coffin lid was half closed, covering Remy's lower body. A few flowers were clustered about the raised lid. Remy's head was propped up on a satin pillow. Her flawless face was covered with thick powder. Red lipstick gleamed on her shapely lips and her cheeks were brightly rouged. Her blonde hair was combed back off her forehead. Despite the heavy makeup, Remy looked pale, ashen. She would have hated the way she looked.

Beneath the makeup, I saw a bruise on Remy's jaw. Her hands, resting on her breast and partially covered by the blanket, revealed red, raw cuts.

She was groomed for eternity. She wore her favorite dance dress, the Cleopatra gold one with the long sleeves, full skirt, and narrow ribbon sash around her waist.

The O'Reillys and I, Remy's daughter and son-in-law, and her ex-husband drove to the National Cemetery in Biloxi. Beau followed in his truck.

Hank and Glenda Smith, who had driven over from Florida, met us at the cemetery. They both hugged me. "Remy had her basketful of trips," Glenda said.

I nodded. I had heard that expression before. Where? Then I remembered. Angela had said that about Dan at his wake.

I was thankful it wasn't raining when Remy was laid to rest. Longfellow's tragic poem, "Evangeline," popped into my mind. Now lovers Dan and Remy slept side by side for all eternity.

There was no funeral feast. Jacquie, her husband, and her father drove directly from Biloxi in separate rented cars to the airport. The Smiths returned to Florida. I stayed overnight with Ellen and Alex, and they drove me to the airport the next morning.

I cried silently all the way back to California. I couldn't believe that Remy was gone forever. She shouldn't have died that way. How could I have missed Remy's affair with Vince? How could I have missed Angela's desperation? Surely I could have done something. I blamed myself. It was too late, way too late.

As the jet banked low around the bay and descended over San Diego's Lindbergh Field, I saw cabs and buses hurrying to and fro and people hastening in every direction. The sun was shining.

EPILOGUE

Crimes of passion or spur-of-the-moment crimes, no matter how heinous, are not considered major crimes in New Orleans. Murders are so commonplace there that they usually go unnoticed, unless the victim is a tourist or a foreigner. Traditionally, murder cases are settled quietly. The suspects, no matter how obvious their guilt, are rarely charged.

The Big Easy has one of the highest murder rates per capita in the United States. In fact, in 1994, New Orleans had the dubious role as murder capital of the United States, racking up 300 murders.

Angela Santorini was charged with second-degree murder. At the preliminary hearing, the judge dismissed the case, calling it a crime of passion. He cited mitigating circumstances: Vangie was 69 years old; she had no criminal record, other than driving under the influence of alcohol; and she was a native New Orleanean. Additionally, I suspected, some powerful, well-connected people in the New Orleans jazz world made sure the case was hushed up.

Angela's only punishment was that she could not leave the State of Louisiana for the rest of her life. Who couldn't live with that sentence? She got away with murder.

I still grieve for my friend whose life ended senselessly, too soon. As I said early on, this was Vince's story. He's alive today because Remy died for him.

CHICKEN JAMBALAYA

¾ cup cooking oil	2 medium onions, chopped
2 green peppers, chopped	½ pound ham, cubed
1 can (16 oz) tomatoes	½ tsp powdered thyme
or equivalent fresh	1 can (6 oz) tomato paste
tomatoes, peeled and seeded	½ cup water, if necessary
4 cups cooked rice	6 green onions, chopped
1 chicken cut in serving pieces	½ pound sausage, sliced
2 cloves garlic, minced	2 sprigs parsley
2 bay leaves	½ to 1 tsp Tabasco sauce

Heat oil in skillet, brown chicken pieces on all sides, remove from pan. Add onions, green onions, peppers, garlic to skillet and cook until onions are transparent. Remove. Add sausage and ham. Saute until sausage is cooked. Add tomato pieces, tomato paste, reserved vegetables and seasonings. Stir in cooked rice gradually until thoroughly mixed, adding water if mixture is too dry. Place rice mixture in baking dish and top with browned chicken pieces. Cover so mixture will not dry out. Bake 2 hours at 350F.

MARDI GRAS RICE*

This is a colorful dish to serve even if it isn't Mardi Gras season. Cut up red, green, and yellow bell peppers and red onions. Saute them lightly in margarine and stir into freshly cooked rice. Lightly dust top with paprika.

MARDI GRAS SALAD

Wash a head of lettuce well, dry and tear into pieces. Slice one yellow bell pepper into long narrow strips. Wash $1/8$ of a head of purple cabbage, drain well and slice into long thin pieces. Serve with Creole Mustard Salad Dressing or Remoulade Sauce.

CREOLE MUSTARD SALAD DRESSING

Blend 2 tablespoons Creole mustard, 2 tablespoons red wine or sherry vinegar, one small onion, peeled and quartered, add salt and pepper to taste in a blender. Slowly pour in oil while blending. Arrange salad with lettuce in bottom of a bowl and purple cabbage and yellow bell pepper strips scattered over the top. Pour ¾ cup dressing over salad. Mardi Gras colors.

*Mardi Gras Rice, Salad, and Dressing are recipes from the Cookin' Cajun Cooking School, New Orleans.

REMY'S QUICK RED BEANS AND RICE

Vegetable cooking spray   2 cloves garlic, minced
The trinity: ½ cup chopped onion, ½ cup chopped celery, and
  ½ cup chopped green pepper
2 cans (15oz each) red kidney beans, drained
½ pound cooked lowfat turkey sausage cut into 1/4-inch slices
2 (8oz) cans tomato sauce   1 tsp Worcestershire sauce
¼ tsp ground red cayenne pepper
¼ tsp Tabasco sauce
3 cups hot cooked rice

Coat a Dutch oven or large heavy pot with cooking spray and place it over medium-high heat until hot. Add onion, celery, green pepper, and garlic. Cook 2 to 3 minutes. Add beans, sausage, tomato sauce, Worcestershire sauce, cayenne pepper, and Tabasco. Reduce heat, cover and simmer 15 minutes. Serve with rice. Serves 6.

ELLEN'S SHRIMP CREOLE

¼ cup all-purpose flour

3 tbl vegetable oil

½ cup chopped green onions

1 cup chopped green pepper

1 tsp dried thyme

2 tsp salt

1 6oz can tomato paste

1 8oz can tomato sauce

4 pounds medium shrimp,
  shelled and deveined

½ cup chopped fresh parsley

1 tbl bacon drippings

2 cups chopped onion

2 garlic cloves, minced

1 cup chopped celery with leaves

2 bay leaves

½ tsp freshly ground black pepper

1 (16oz) can tomatoes

1 cup fish stock or water

1 tsp tabasco sauce

1 tbl fresh lemon juice

2 cups cooked rice

In a Dutch oven or large, heavy pan over medium heat, stir the flour, drippings, and oil until the roux becomes a deep, red-brown, about 30 minutes. Add the onion, green onions, garlic, green pepper, celery, thyme, bay leaves, salt and black pepper. Cook, stirring constantly, until onion is transparent and soft, about 20 minutes. Add the tomato paste and cook for 3 minutes. Chop the tomatoes and add them, with their liquid, the tomato sauce, and the stock. Simmer, partially covered for 1 hour, stirring occasionally.

Add the shrimp and cook until they are done, about 5 minutes. Stir in the Tabasco sauce, parsley, and lemon juice. Cover and remove from heat. This dish is best when allowed to stand several hours or overnight in the refrigerator. Reheat, without boiling, and serve over rice.

SHELLFISH BOIL

Heat water in a 10-gallon pot over an outdoor fire. Buy commercial Crab Boil, a mixture of peppercorns, bay leaves, and other herbs, and follow directions on the box. Cut several lemons in half and throw in the pot. Add corn on the cob, cut in half, baby new potatoes, and small whole onions, all of which pick up the flavor of the Crab Boil seasoning. Cook crawfish until they are bright red (about 15 minutes), crabs (about 10 minutes), and shrimp until they turn pink (about 5 minutes). Spread newspapers or brown paper on a wooden picnic table and serve hot right out of the pot. Everyone peels their favorite shellfish and makes a mess to their hearts content. Afterwards, just roll up the papers and discard them in a plastic bag in the trash can.

SEAFOOD GUMBO

1 recipe roux	3 cups dry white wine
2 large onions, finely chopped	3 cups water
2 large garlic cloves,	2 tsp Tabasco sauce
finely chopped	2 tbl Worcestershire Sauce
1 medium bell pepper,	1 pint fresh oysters
finely chopped	½ box frozen okra,
2 pounds peeled	discard ends and slice
shrimp Gumbo filé	

2 or 3 crabs in pieces, discard back shell

Make roux from 1-½ cups sifted flour, 1 small can tomato sauce, 1 small can tomato paste, and 3/4 cup olive oil. Cover bottom of heavy 6-quart pot with olive oil. Heat over low fire and add flour. Cook slowly, stirring continuously. The flour should be very dark brown but not burned. Add 1 can tomato paste, stirring until roux is color of paste. Add sauce and repeat process for about an hour. Mixture should be dark brown.

Add to roux chopped onions, garlic, and bell pepper. Keep stirring. Add equal parts of wine and water until mixture is the consistency of thick soup. Add Tabasco and Worcestershire sauces. Bring to boil. Add raw shrimp, oysters, sliced okra. Cook over slow heat about 2 hours. Boil crab. Discard back shell and break into pieces, bodies, and claws. Add bodies and claws to gumbo and serve with rice and filé powder (added at the last minute).

ANDOUILLE ISLANDS*

Fry thick slices of Andouille sausage on both sides until well browned. Fry eggs in a separate skillet. Place three eggs on a plate, sunnyside up and place three slices of Andouille between the eggs. Garnish with slice of orange and parsley. Serve with hash brown potatoes, parslied grits, fruit, and biscuits.

*From The Cabin Restaurant, Burnside, Louisiana

BEAU'S QUICK CAJUN CATFISH

⅓ cup skim buttermilk	1-1/2 tsp dried thyme
2 tsp Dijon mustard	½ tsp Cayenne pepper
½ cup cornmeal	½ tsp freshly ground black pepper
½ tsp garlic powder	1 tsp paprika
4 catfish fillets (1-¼ pounds)	4 lemon wedges
1 tsp salt	1 tsp onion powder

Preheat broiler or get the grill really hot. Lightly oil a wire rack large enough to hold fish in a single layer. Put rack on baking sheet and set aside.

In a medium-sized bowl, whisk together buttermilk and mustard until smooth. In a shallow dish, combine cornmeal, salt, and spices. Dip each fillet in the buttermilk mixture, turning to coat. Transfer to the cornmeal mixture, turning to coat completely. Place the fillets on the prepared rack. They should not touch. Broil 4 inches from the heat source or grill until fish are opaque in the center, about 3 minutes per side. Serve hot with lemon wedges. Serves 4.

SHRIMP JAMBALAYA

2 lbs raw whole shrimp	1 cup raw rice
1 cup diced ham	3 bay leaves
½ cup chopped onion	Salt
¼ cup chopped celery	2 tbs butter
2 cups tomatoes	Cayenne pepper
¼ cup chopped green pepper	2 garlic cloves

Sauce onion, green pepper, celery, garlic in melted butter. Add shrimp and ham, fry 5 minutes. Stir in tomatoes, cook 10 minutes. Stir in rice, add seasonings and 1 cup water. Bring to boil. Cover, simmer until rice is done, about 30 minutes.

MARY MAHONEY'S BREAD PUDDING

6 slices day-old bread	2 tbl melted butter
2 tbl plus ½ cup sugar	½ cup seedless raisins
1 tsp cinnamon	1 tsp vanilla extract
4 eggs	2 cups milk

Break bread in small pieces in baking dish, about 1-½ quart size. Sprinkle cinnamon over bread and add raisins and melted butter. Toast lightly bread mixture in oven about 350 F. Then add mixture of eggs, sugar, milk, and vanilla. Mix well. Bake about 30 minutes or until solid. Serves 8.

RUM SAUCE

2 cups milk	½ stick butter
½ cup sugar	1 tbl nutmeg
1 tbl vanilla Rum or bourbon to taste	

Place milk, butter, and sugar in sauce pan. Bring to boil, thicken with a roux made of 2 tablespoons flour and 1 tablespoon oil. Remove from fire, add nutmeg, vanilla, and rum or bourbon to taste. Serve over bread pudding.

SHRIMP REMOULADE SALAD

In a bowl, arrange a bed of crisp curly lettuce pieces. Pile cold boiled shrimp, peeled, in the center, surrounded by cucumber slices, cut tomatoes, pepper rings, and lemon slices. You may garnish with hard-boiled egg wedges around the outside. Drizzle Remoulade Sauce over top.

REMOULADE SAUCE*

1 medium onion	2 tsp salt
1 bunch green onions	½ cup Creole mustard
1 stalk celery	2 tbl lemon juice
2 cloves garlic	2 tbl vinegar
¼ cup parsley	1 tbl Worcestershire Sauce
1 tbl paprika	4 shakes Tabasco Sauce
1/4 tsp Cayenne pepper	¾ cup vegetable oil

Combine all ingredients except oil in food processor. Turn on and slowly dribble in the oil. Allow flavors to marry for 24 hours or at least half an hour. Season to taste.

*From Bobby Potts' Cookbook, "Cookin' Country Cajun."